LIVING GOD'S WAY

Living God's Way

A Course for Discipling New Christians

ARTHUR WALLIS

KINGSWAY PUBLICATIONS
EASTBOURNE

First published 1984
Reprinted 1984
Reprinted 1985
Reprinted 1986
Reprinted 1988
Reprinted 1990
Reprinted 1992

ISBN 0 86065 280 7

Biblical quotations are from the
New International Version, © New York International
Bible Society 1978

Front cover photo: Photo Library International Ltd

Printed in Great Britain for
KINGSWAY PUBLICATIONS LTD
1 St Anne's Road, Eastbourne, E. Sussex BN21 3UN by
Clays Ltd, St Ives plc.
Typeset by Nuprint Ltd, Harpenden, Herts.

Contents

Introduction

1 A Word about the Course

This course has been designed for use in a local church setting where the new Christian is being *personally* discipled, not necessarily by a leader or recognized teacher in the church, but simply by another believer older in the faith. This method will result in the greatest benefit both for the disciple and the teacher.

It could involve couples discipling couples as well as an individual brother or sister, married or single, discipling another of the same sex. I have tried to keep the language and concepts simple, so that it should be quite possible for an older teenager to disciple another teenager, or for Christian parents to use the course with their teenage children.

Perhaps you question the rightness of someone who is not a leader teaching someone else. The letter to the Hebrews was not written to church leaders but to believers in general. The author rebuked them for their slowness to learn, telling them, 'Though by this time *you ought to be teachers*, you need someone to teach you the elementary truths of God's word all over again' (5:11–12). It is clear from the New Testament that believers in general are expected to 'teach and admonish one another' (Col 3:16).

Sadly, our churches are full of believers, like the Hebrew Christians just mentioned, who are more in need of being taught the basics of the faith than being able to teach others. I am hopeful that the 'disciplers' will get as much from this course as those they disciple.

We have come to an exciting day of evangelistic endeavour. The fields are surely 'ripe for harvest'. There is a growing expectation for the outpouring of the Holy Spirit, with the massive ingathering that that would bring. But are our churches ready? Not if they are only prepared for conversions by the handful instead of by the hundreds and thousands.

It will be nothing short of a tragedy if, with a record catch on our hands, the nets break and the catch is lost. The remedy is within our grasp. Alongside the current emphasis on every-member evangelism we must be prepared for every-member discipling. The call to rank and file believers to teach others is not beyond their spiritual capabilities. I believe hundreds of Christians, frustrated by a feeling that they are of little worth, or weighed down with personal problems, could find a new release and great fulfilment as 'a teacher of infants' in the faith (Rom 2:20).

Personal discipling is not without its dangers, but these can be overcome if it is done in a church setting, and carefully monitored by the elders. More of this aspect later. While not discounting the value of a small group going through the course together, the advantages of the one-to-one method are:

1. As soon as converted the new disciple can begin the course without waiting for a new 'converts class' to commence.

2. The course can proceed at the speed suitable for the convert, and can adjust for delays owing to holidays, sickness, etc.

3. There is an intimacy and a friendship that can develop

between teacher and disciple. The convert will be more ready to open up on personal needs and problems.

4. That first audible prayer comes much more easily in such a setting than in a house group or converts' class.

The emphasis of the course is practical. The pressing need in the first days of the Christian life is teaching that relates to the business of 'living God's way' in an alien society. Although the course is full of Scripture, the emphasis is practical rather than simply doctrinal.

There is some homework with each of the studies. However, this is not of the usual variety: a question, a scripture reference and a blank to fill in, where it is possible to score 'ten out of ten' without making any spiritual progress! The questions will require the disciple to apply the lessons to his or her own life, and will usually necessitate having direct dealings with God over the issues raised. And when the teacher and disciple meet for the next study they can go over this ground together. This should help the person teaching to know how much truth is really sinking in and what real spiritual progress is being made.

2 A Word to the Disciple

Welcome to this course of study. If you are a new Christian, may I say how delighted I am to know that you are now a part of God's family, and to greet you as a brother or sister in Christ. I believe that God will make the course a great blessing to you. Twenty sessions may seem a formidable task to face, but you will be free to take it at your own speed, and you should discuss this frankly with your teacher.

There was a parable told by Jesus about two builders. The wise one built his house on the rock, and when the storm came it stood firm. The foolish one built his house on the sand, and when the storm came it collapsed. Let's apply this to you, in the way Jesus did to his hearers. Whether you, as his disciple, are the wise or foolish builder, depends on *whether or not you hear and obey* what Jesus says. This course will help you to learn what Christ wants from his disciples, and then it will help and encourage you to obey. Look upon it as a foundation-laying course for your Christian life.

Many commit their lives to Christ, but never become firm and secure in their faith. Others sadly give up altogether when temptations assail. They make the mistake of never paying attention to their spiritual foundations. Laying them is a demanding and time-consuming task. But because you're building a house that you're going to occupy, your own safety and security depends on the foundations. How glad was the wise man in the middle of the night when he heard the wind howling and the flood waters rising, that he had taken all that trouble over the foundations.

If this good news about Jesus is something completely new to you, you will find your teacher a great help in grasping some of the truths, in finding your way around the Bible, and in facing some of the practical difficulties of 'living God's way' in our modern world. We have all had to face these same battles. That's where we are able to help one another. Before very long *you* should be able to help another new Christian in the same way that you have been helped. That's exciting, isn't it? All that you will require for the course is your own copy of this study manual, your own copy of the Bible (preferably the New International Version [NIV] on which the course is based; quite inexpensive editions are available), a notebook for the home tasks and something to write with.

The course is divided into three sections, each having an introduction explaining the ground to be covered.

Similarly, each study has its own introduction. Read this before you meet with your teacher. If you can also read in advance the study itself, in order to get the gist of it, that will be a great help.

One of the main purposes of the course is to teach you to talk to God yourself about the things that he is saying to you, and to learn to listen to his voice. The home task is geared for this, and is therefore very practical. Do these diligently, recording any answers in your notebook. Be ready to share your findings with your teacher when you next meet.

With each study there is also a verse to memorize. I have found the memorizing of Scripture a great blessing in my service for God, and I would encourage you in this. But if it's more than you can cope with, forget it. For those who do want to do it, may I suggest that you write out the verses on small cards. If you prefer to memorize in a version more familiar to you than the NIV, then do that. And as you proceed, keep refreshing your memory on the ones already learned. Continual rehearsing is the secret of memorizing. And don't forget to include the scripture reference.

At the end of this introduction to the course is a list of abbreviations of the books of the Bible and versions of the Bible used in the notes. You may need to refer to these when looking up scripture references.

It now remains for me to commit you to God and to his word which can build you up in your Christian faith, and make you strong in Christ. God bless you.

3 A Word to the Teacher

May I welcome you also to this course as a teacher. To be called to share with someone else what you have learned about how to live God's way is an exciting and demanding task. Be assured that God is with you, and will give you all the wisdom and strength you need as you look to him in faith. Let me share with you some key things to help you to make the sessions as fruitful as possible.

If you are leading someone through this course in a church setting, there should be an elder or other mature leader appointed to oversee your discipling. If this has been overlooked, speak to your leaders and ask for a particular leader to take this responsibility. You and your disciple will both feel more secure in the knowledge that you are covered in this way, especially if you run into problems that you feel unable to handle.

Before you undertake any discipling take time to *go right through the course*, looking up the scripture references, and ensuring that you are clear about the truths being taught. Paul has a word for the person who aspires to be 'a teacher of infants'—and that's what everyone is who disciples a new Christian. He says, 'You, then, who teach others, do you not teach yourself?' (Rom 2:21). In other words, you must be 'practising what you preach'. There are parts of the course that you will find a challenge to your own Christian life, so remember you will communicate to your disciple not only what you say, but what you are.

There's another important reason for going right through the course before you commence. You can note anything that you yourself do not fully understand and talk it through with your elder. That's much better than being caught out in the middle of a study! Better still, perhaps your church could run a training seminar and go right through the material with all those who are to be involved in discipling.

A key to the progress of the one you are discipling will be the relationship that is established between you. Make it one of true friendship. It is not difficult to receive and respond to instruction when you know that the one giving it really loves you and is wholly for you. Take time to find out about his or her background, family, interests, conversion to Christ, present struggles, etc. Not only will this express your loving concern, but enable you to pray for your disciple intelligently and apply the teaching in the most helpful way. Why not have a meal together before you start the course proper, or at least set apart some time to get acquainted? It is equally important that you share about yourself, and how you came to Christ.

As you go through the studies together, encourage your new Christian to pray with you out loud—even if at first it's only a one-sentence prayer. Teach your disciple to talk to God in an easy conversational way, and in the language that they would use with any other friend. Before moving on to the new study check the home task from the previous study. Encourage the disciple to share his (or her) findings, and talk through any difficulties encountered. Your concern is to know whether he (or she) has entered into the good of what you have taught.

Now you are ready to read through the introduction to the new study together and work through the teaching, helping your disciple to look up the scripture references, and to understand what God is saying. A list of the Bible books with their abbreviations found at the commencement of the course will help here. Watch that you don't get sidetracked on to some other interesting related topic. This may prolong the time unduly. Keep it for discussion at the end, if time permits.

It is very important to share your own experience, as it relates to the theme of the study, even experiences of failure, and how God brought you through into victory. The new Christian will identify with this and be encouraged.

Pray much over these times together. Ask God continually to enable you to impart the truth in a spirit of faith, so that your new Christian will also receive it in a spirit of faith, and start to walk in it. Otherwise the burden on the disciple of all that he (or she) is required to do will appear to get bigger and bigger, without a realization of the grace that is available to make it work.

It is important that you report regularly to the elder concerned as to how you are progressing. In the Community Church here in Southampton, where we have a number already going through the course, we have drafted a simple monthly progress report, with an account of each study completed, and an end-of-the-month report on general progress made.

Finally, remember the fellow Christians, leaders and others, who have had a part in shaping your Christian life, and bringing you thus far along the road. God is now going to use you to shape another life for eternity. What a privilege! Give yourself to the task humbly, prayerfully and conscientiously—and God be with you.

4 Abbreviations

Scripture references

Genesis	Gen
Exodus	Ex
Leviticus	Lev
Numbers	Num
Deuteronomy	Deut
Joshua	Josh
Judges	Judg
Ruth	Ruth
1 and 2 Samuel	1 and 2 Sam
1 and 2 Kings	1 and 2 Kings
1 and 2 Chronicles	1 and 2 Chron
Ezra	Ezra
Nehemiah	Neh
Esther	Esther
Job	Job

Psalms	Ps
Proverbs	Prov
Ecclesiastes	Eccles
Song of Solomon	Song
Isaiah	Is
Jeremiah	Jer
Lamentations	Lam
Ezekiel	Ezek
Daniel	Dan
Hosea	Hos
Joel	Joel
Amos	Amos
Obadiah	Obad
Jonah	Jon
Micah	Mic
Nahum	Nahum
Habakkuk	Hab
Zephaniah	Zeph
Haggai	Hag
Zechariah	Zech
Malachi	Mal
Matthew	Mt
Mark	Mk
Luke	Lk
John	Jn
Acts	Acts
Romans	Rom
1 and 2 Corinthians	1 and 2 Cor
Galatians	Gal
Ephesians	Eph
Philippians	Phil
Colossians	Col
1 and 2 Thessalonians	1 and 2 Thess
1 and 2 Timothy	1 and 2 Tim
Titus	Tit
Philemon	Philem
Hebrews	Heb
James	Jas
1 and 2 Peter	1 and 2 Pet

1, 2 and 3 John	1, 2, and 3 Jn
Jude	Jude
Revelation	Rev

Note: 'a' or 'b' at the end of a reference indicates that only the first or second half of the verse is meant, for example, Eph 2:3a or Col 2:6b; 'f' or 'ff' at the end of a reference indicates that the verse (f) (or verses ff) following should also be read.

Bible versions

AV	The Authorized (or King James) Version
RSV	Revised Standard Version
NASB	New American Standard Bible
Phillips	*The New Testament in Modern English* by J. B. Phillips
NIV	New International Version

Coming into Christ

(Studies 1—6)

In ancient times if you wanted to qualify for membership of certain secret societies there were rites and ceremonies that you had to go through. Some of these were things that were done to you, while others were things that you had to be willing to do yourself. Only then did you fully belong. You had been 'initiated' into that society. Christianity is not a free for all. There is what we might call 'Christian initiation'. The heart of this is, of course, the new birth, on coming into Christ. Though you may have experienced this, it is essential that you understand clearly what has happened to you. But there are other things too that are not optional extras, such as water baptism and the fullness of the Holy Spirit. These are essential if you want to enjoy the full privileges of the kingdom of God. This part of the course will deal with the foundations of your Christian life. It is so important that you get these right.

Introducing Study 1

THE BIG CHANGE

The Bible calls it conversion, being saved or being born again. To understand what God has done in you and for you we must first take a glance back and recall *how you were* before the big change took place. It's not a question of how you then saw yourself, or how your relatives or friends saw you, but how *God* saw you. That, and only that, is how you really were. Then we must look at what God says *you are now*. That means looking at your new spiritual identity. You are not yet what you will be. But nor are you what you once were. A miracle has taken place inside you. It's not that you decided to become 'religious', go straight or turn over a new leaf—and keeping your fingers crossed that you will be able to keep it up! God has made you a brand-new person. It's not that you necessarily *feel* tremendously different. It's not a matter of feelings but of facts. It's because you *are* different you have begun to live differently—to live God's way.

This study has more than the usual number of scriptural references to look up. Don't be daunted by this. The study itself is not difficult, and getting accustomed to finding your way around the Bible is an important aspect of the course.

STUDY 1

The Big Change

Read 2 Corinthians 5:14–21

Sin and its cause. It's a disease that all men have contracted (Rom 3:23). 'Fall short' is like an arrow not reaching the target. 'A miss is as good as a mile'. All of us have failed to measure up to God's standard of righteousness, called here 'the glory of God'. Our good deeds cannot make up for our failures. Even our good deeds are not acceptable to God (Is 64:6). Men are not sinners because they sin, but they sin because they are sinners, i.e. were born with a sinful nature (Ps 51:5). As sheep have an inborn tendency to go astray, we have an inborn tendency to do our own thing and go our own way (Is 53:6).

'*The old has gone, the new has come!*' (2 Cor 5:17) is the key to what has happened to you:

The old has gone

Before you came to Christ you chose darkness. You were therefore responsible for the state you were in, and quite helpless to put it right. The Bible says you were:

    1. Dead (Eph 2:1), that is, unable to respond to God, to obey God or to please God.

    2. Defiled because sin is spiritual uncleanness. The

body may be clean while the mind and the conscience are corrupted or defiled (Tit 1:15).

3. *Enslaved* by sin, and unable to get free (Jn 8:34), 'enslaved by all kinds of passions and pleasures' (Tit 3:3).

4. *Blinded* by Satan (2 Cor 4:4), and so unable to 'see' the truth.

5. *Under God's judgement* with the threat of divine punishment hanging over your head, because God was angry about your sin (Eph 2:3b).

6. *Cut off from God* 'Separate from Christ...without God...far away' (Eph 2:12–13), like the lost (prodigal) son in the far country (Lk 15:13). If you had not repented and received Christ this separation would have resulted in eternal death (Rom 6:23), that is, hell.

The new has come

Though you may have the same physical appearance, temperament and personality, you have become a brand-new person, 'a new creation', with new attitudes, new relationships, new outlook, new purpose in life, new interests and new friends. 'The big change' is described as being:

1. *Forgiven* (1 Jn 1:9a). When God forgives he also forgets (Is 43:25). Don't let your memory condemn you (Rom 8:1, 33–34). The burden has lifted.

2. *Justified*, or declared righteous before God (Rom 3:24). At the cross Jesus took your sin that you might take his righteousness (2 Cor 5:21). What a wonderful exchange!

3. *Cleansed*. Mind, memory, imagination and conscience are purified through Christ's blood (1 Jn 1:7). Isn't it good to feel clean?

4. *Reconciled*. Before you were God's enemy, now you are his friend (Rom 5:10). You'll never find a friend to compare with him.

5. *Born again* (Jn 3:3). Physical birth gave you the life

of your parents, but this new birth gives you the life of God, eternal life (Jn 10:27–28).

6. *In God's family.* God is now your Father, you are his son or daughter (2 Cor 6:18), and that means all other believers are your brothers and sisters. As Father he is committed to love, protect, provide for, and train you.

7. *Bound for heaven.* Jesus has gone to prepare a place for you (Jn 14:2–3). Meanwhile he is preparing you for that place. The best is yet to come (1 Cor 2:9).

All these are not simply what preachers say, but what God says of you as a true believer.

Memorize: *Therefore, if anyone is in Christ, he is a new creation; the old has gone, the new has come!* (2 Cor 5:17). (Try to memorize the reference as well as the scripture.)

Home task

1. Under the heading 'The Old Has Gone' there are six descriptions of your old life. Look up one scripture under each description and write it out in full in your notebook. Remember, that's how it is with your relatives and friends who are still without Christ. Make a list of them and start asking God to save them as he saved you.

2. Under the heading 'The New Has Come' there are seven descriptions of you as a brand-new person. Find a quiet place on your own. Look up one scripture under each description and *confess out loud* what it says you are, followed by the scripture. For example, the first would be:

'I am *forgiven*, because 1 John 1:9 says, "If we confess our sins" etc.' Then write it out in your notebook before moving on to the next one until you have completed all seven. Finish up with a big thank you session with your Father for all the blessings of this big change in your life.

Introducing Study 2

HAND-PICKED

'How did you find Christ?' someone asked an African Christian. 'I didn't find him,' came the answer, 'he found me!' In salvation God always makes the first move. He was seeking you before you began seeking him. In fact, it all goes back long before the seeking/finding process began. You may have thought that you chose Christ, but that was only because he had first chosen you.

That is the theme of this study. Believers call it 'the doctrine of election'. You may wonder how God could choose you before you were born or had any existence. Or how he could 'elect' you and then give you free will to choose yourself to love and serve him, and no one lives and serves God without choosing to do so. Don't worry. These things have perplexed the minds of the greatest Christians down the centuries. I don't have to understand the laws of electricity to enjoy its benefits. Praise God we don't have to unravel the mystery of election to enjoy the blessing of knowing that God has chosen us simply because he loves us.

Hand-Picked

Read Deuteronomy 7:6–9

God took the first step

Salvation is not man groping after God, but God reaching down to man. The Bible teaches that God chose some men (election), but he gave to all a will to decide and holds them responsible for how they exercise it. The truth lies in both these facts, however difficult it may seem to reconcile them. We are required to believe, not necessarily to understand.

When were you chosen?

It wasn't after you had lived a while and looked a promising candidate for salvation! It was before you were born, and had done anything good or bad (Rom 9:10–12). It was even before the world was created (Eph 1:4).

What was the basis of God's choice?

Since he chose you before you were born it could not be because of your good deeds. It was on the basis of God's mercy and grace (Tit 3:5; 2 Tim 1:9). You will hear a lot about grace on this course. It means God's abounding love towards those who are unworthy of it. 'Something for nothing for those who don't deserve anything.' He chose you because he loved you when there was nothing to love. Did you notice in the reading that that was why he chose Israel (Deut 7:7)?

You were a love gift

You were a love gift from the Father to the Son (Jn 6:37). You came to Jesus, not primarily because you decided to, but because the Father drew you (verse 44). No one comes without that drawing. It is a work of the Holy Spirit.

God didn't get a shock!

In his foreknowledge God knew all about you when he chose you (1 Pet 1:2). Couples marry, only to discover what they've let themselves in for! Despite your weakness, frailty and sinfulness, God wanted you. Out of millions he has chosen you! You are 'special', hand-picked.

Learn to accept yourself

God chose you, created you as he wanted you to be, and now he has redeemed you. Don't crave for someone else's looks, personality, temperament, natural gifts, etc. Having chosen you, God formed you as a person according to his own will and design. Don't question this (Rom 9:20). Instead praise him for it (Ps 139:14).

The pressure is off

You no longer need feel, 'It all depends on me. Have I got what it takes?' Instead, 'It's over to God who chose me, knowing me better than I knew myself. His grace is more than enough for all my needs' (Jn 1:16; 2 Cor 12:9).

God has a perfect plan for you

Choice has to do with purpose. The carpenter chooses a tool with a job in mind. God didn't save you, and then wonder what to do with you. He chose you for a purpose, and when you were saved that set the plan in motion (Eph 2:10) You may not know what that plan is, but God will unfold it step by step. As you carry out that plan you will not only be secure, but fruitful and fulfilled (Jn 15:16).

Memorize: *For it is by grace you have been saved, through faith—and this is not from yourselves, it is the gift of God—not by works, so that no-one can boast* (Eph 2:8–9).

Home task

Use your notebook to answer these questions:

1. What are the wonderful things that should result from the fact that God has chosen you? See Ephesians 1:4 and Romans 8:29.

2. What are the four wonderful things that 1 Peter 2:9 says God's people are because he has chosen us?

3. Jot down all *the things that you like* about the way God has made you. Then list *the things (if any) you don't like*, or wish were different. Then thank him for *all* of them, and tell him, 'Father, you have done all things well.'

Introducing Study 3

WHAT GOD DID

In the last study we said that salvation did not begin with you but with God. He chose you because he loved you. Now we must consider what he did to express his love and to make his choice effective and meaningful.

We will not be thinking so much of what God has done *in* you by making you a new creature in Christ, which we called 'the big change' (Study 1), but what he has done *for* you in sending Jesus into the world to be your Saviour. We shall be thinking about the basis of salvation, the great historic event of the cross and its meaning. Why was it necessary for Jesus to come? Why did he have to die? How can we be sure that his death and resurrection have accomplished anything? It is so important that you understand this. God's act of choosing you could not in itself restore you to himself. The cause of separation between him and you had to be removed. He had to find a way of justifying you while remaining himself a just and holy God.

STUDY 3

What God Did

Read Romans 5:1–9

The problem of sin

God made man to enjoy fellowship with him, but sin brought estrangement (Gen 3:8). How could there ever again be fellowship? Only by the cause of the estrangement being removed. Man was 'powerless' to do anything about it (Rom 5:6). It would have been like trying to lift himself up by tugging on his bootlaces. Only God could deal with the problem.

The solution

Though God loved you and chose you, he could not disregard your sin (Hab 1:13a). Sin always has to be paid for. You were bankrupt, so God paid the sum himself so you could be forgiven your debt. How did God do it?

Blood must be shed

When God planned to redeem Israel from Egyptian slavery a lamb had to be sacrificed by every household (Ex 12:3ff). This pointed forward to 'the Lamb of God' who was to come (Jn 1:29). Later God taught Israel that there could not be forgiveness without the shedding of blood (Heb 9:22b). Since the law of God insists that the penalty of your sin is death (Ezek 18:4), Jesus, the only sinless man, had to suffer to save you from your sin and bring you back to God (1 Pet 3:18a). It is only through the blood of Jesus that you are cleansed from your sin (1 Jn 1:7b).

Justified by his blood

Did you notice that the word 'justified' came twice in your reading? Justification is the act by which God declares sinful men righteous. Verse 1 says that you are 'justified by faith'. That's your side of it, and we shall be looking at that more particularly in the next study. But verse 9 says that you are 'justified by his blood'. That's God's side of it. In the matter of righteousness you were declared bankrupt. But Jesus came and discharged your debts on the cross. All his righteousness was paid into your account.

How can you be sure?

The proof that God accepted the sacrifice of Jesus to justify you is seen in the fact that he raised him from the dead (Rom 4:25). Sometimes, after a man's death, the terms of his will are not carried out. Jesus, when he died, left you a legacy of salvation. Then he rose again to make sure you got it! (1 Pet 1:3–4.) Now he's in heaven ensuring that all the terms of the will are carried out.

His love—your response

The cross of Jesus is the supreme act of God's love (Rom 5:8). The man in the dock, so the story goes, was found guilty. The judge, though an old friend, didn't treat the offence lightly. He fined him as heavily as he could, and

28

then handed him a cheque for the full sum. Because God was holy he had to punish sin with the sentence of death. At the cross God the Judge stepped down from the bench and paid your debt in the blood of Jesus. That's what grace is all about. What should your response be? In his great hymn, Isaac Watts wrote, 'Love so amazing, so divine, demands my soul, my life my all'. See Paul's response in Phil 3:7–9.

Memorize: *For God so loved the world that he gave his one and only Son, that whoever believes in him shall not perish but have eternal life* (Jn 3:16).

Home task

Use your notebook to register your answers to the following questions:

1. The fact that Christ died and rose again entitles him to what position in your life? (Rom 14:9.)

2. What do you think that means in practical terms? Include in your answer the areas of your life that ought to be affected by this.

Introducing Study 4

WHAT YOU DID

In the last lesson we saw how God, having set his love on you, took action to free you from your sin and bring you to himself. But salvation, as you well know, is not a work that God carries out independently of us; it requires our willing response and co-operation.

A Christian was talking to a soap manufacturer about his faith. 'Don't think much of your Christianity,' he said to the Christian. 'It's been around all these centuries, and look at the mess the human race is in.' At this point they passed two or three children playing in the mud at the side of the road. 'What about your soap?' replied the Christian. 'It's been around longer than Christianity, but look at the mess those kids are in.' 'Ah,' retorted the manufacturer, 'my soap is only effective as and when it is applied.' 'That's exactly how it is with Christianity' came the answer.

In this study we shall be looking at the question of how the work that Christ has done for us is personally applied. It is important that we check out the whole area of our responsibility.

What You Did

Read Acts 20:17–21

Introduction

If Christ died for all, why are not all saved? Though salvation is *sufficient* for all, it is only *effective* for those who respond in the right way to the good news. Remember the story of the judge who fined his friend? What would have happened if the convicted man had torn up the cheque? As well as the work that God performs in salvation, Scripture emphasizes the part that we are required to play in salvation. We must always *work out* what God *works in* (Phil 2:12–13).

Acts of the will

Mind, emotions and will are all involved. When a man hears the good news his *mind* may be convinced, his *emotions* may be stirred, but if his *will* is not moved he is not converted. The lost son said, '*I will* set out and go back to my father' (Lk 15:18), and that was the turning point in his life. 'Whosoever *will*, let him take' (Rev 22:17, AV). In conversion this decision of the will must be expressed in *repentance* towards God, *faith* in our Lord Jesus and *confession* towards men. Let's look carefully at these actions.

Repentance

'Turn to God in repentance' (Acts 20:21). The word means 'a change of mind'. Instead of rejecting or ignoring God, we turn to him in acknowledgement of who he is. That will also mean a change of mind about ourselves, that we *are* sinners and *need* salvation. It's more than just thinking 'I'm wrong', or saying 'I'm sorry'. It's *a change of mind that leads to a change of course*. A father and son were living in a log cabin. The son took no notice of the father's repeated request to fetch logs and stoke the fire. Father: 'You either fetch those logs or quit this place!' The son stormed out. Weeks later he returned weak and hungry. Son: 'Dad, I'm sorry'. Father: 'All right, son, then fetch those logs' (Cf. Mt 21:28–29). There must be 'fruit in keeping with repentance' (Mt 3:8). Repentance must be followed by *confession* of our sin to God and *forsaking* it (Prov 28:13). If others have been wronged we must confess to them too. Damage must be made good, e.g. money or goods stolen must be restored with interest (Lk 19:8).

Faith

'Have faith in our Lord Jesus' (Acts 20:21). Most people are trusting to their 'good deeds'. 'Are you a Christian?' 'I hope so, I'm doing my best.' This fosters pride. Salvation is a gift, not a wage or a reward (Rom 6:23). It is received by faith, not worked for (Eph 2:8–9). Faith is not simply a mental acceptance. Believing *about* Christ is not the same as believing *in* him. 'I believe *about* Satan, but *not in* him' (Cf. Jas 2:19). Believing in Christ is a thing of the heart more than the head (Rom 10:10) and it leads to committing myself to him. If I am unwilling to commit myself and *submit* myself to him to rule over me, I haven't really *believed in him*. True believing always results in 'calling on the Lord' (Rom 10:13).

Confession

This completes the process. To confess Christ is to let other people know that you side with Christ as your Saviour and Lord (Rom 10:9–10). This often has a profound effect on unbelievers and may lead to their salvation. It always gladdens the heart of Christ, and he then confesses your name before his Father (Mt 10:32).

Memorize: *He who conceals his sins does not prosper, but whoever confesses and renounces them finds mercy* (Prov 28:13).

Home task

The Bible says 'Make your calling and election sure' (2 Pet 1:10), and 'Examine yourselves to see whether you are in the faith' (2 Cor 13:5). This will either confirm us in the faith or save us from thinking that we are all right when we are not.

1. Review your past life before you came to Christ, and ask yourself, 'Have I renounced and forsaken all that I know to be sin?' Call on God for grace to deal with any areas in which you are not yet clear.

2. Ask yourself, 'Have I really committed myself to Jesus Christ?' Is he really Lord of every part of my life? Again, take to him in prayer those areas over which he is not yet ruling.

3. If then, you are still having a struggle over certain matters, share them with the one who is discipling you for his (or her) counsel and prayer. Be assured, God has chosen you to be free.

Introducing Study 5

BAPTISM IN WATER

We have now completed our study of that work of God in us called 'the new birth'. But there are still other matters that are part and parcel of our coming into Christ and which, therefore, belong to this opening section. They are of great importance in our new life in Christ. The first is the rite of water baptism.

Although it might appear a simple outward act or just a religious ceremony, baptism is an act of the utmost importance and significance for us. It not only speaks of what has happened to us now that we have come into Christ, but it is also designed to 'trigger off' faith in us for the future, to live from now on in the full blessing of our salvation. In non-Christian lands people don't always take a lot of notice when a person of another religion professes to believe in Christ, but when he (or she) follows this by being baptized the opposition breaks out. Everybody understands that baptism is the outward sign that you mean business.

As you read the New Testament epistles you will find that nowhere are believers exhorted to get baptized. It is taken for granted that this happened when they were born again. We don't come across any unbaptized Christians in the New Testament churches. If you are *not* yet baptized, this study will help you to see the importance of obeying this command of Christ. If you *are* baptized, this will help you to understand more perfectly what has happened, and what should result from it.

Baptism in Water

Read Romans 6:1–11

Introduction

Because of confusion and controversy among Christians about baptism, we need to be clear as to what the Bible teaches. The question is *not* 'What does *church tradition* say?' but 'What does *the Scripture* say?' (Gal 4:30). There is no confusion or uncertainty about it if we rely on Scripture alone. It tells us how baptism is to be practised and what it really means.

Babes or believers?

The only infants baptized in the New Testament were 'babes' in Christ (i.e. newly 'born again' believers). Baptism in Scripture always *follows* repentance and faith (Mk 16:16; Acts 2:38). It was *after* a person became a disciple that he was to be baptized (Mt 28:19). We never find the order reversed.

It is by immersion

Baptizo (Greek) translated 'baptize' means literally to

dip, immerse, submerge. New Testament believers were, therefore, *immersed*. So John needed plenty of water to do the job (Jn 3:23). This is confirmed by the description of Jesus' baptism. He came 'up out of the water' (Mk 1:10). So with Philip and the eunuch (Acts 8:38–39).

Who should do it?

A responsible person, but not necessarily holding a position of leadership. Jesus did not personally baptize, but left it to his followers (Jn 4:2). If a believer is able to disciple another he should be qualified to baptize him (Mt 28:19). The great apostle Paul was baptized by one simply described as 'a disciple' (Acts 9:10, 18).

What does it mean?

1. I've been initiated. Baptism is a ceremony of initiation (admission to membership). We are not baptized 'into a denomination', but 'into Christ' (Rom 6:3), and thus into his body, the church.

2. I've been sealed. It's like circumcision was to Abraham, 'a seal of the righteousness that he had by faith' (Rom 4:11). It should confirm and strengthen your faith. Let's say, here's a letter representing *you*, and an envelope representing *Christ*. The letter is placed in the envelope, just as in conversion you are placed in Christ. Then the envelope is sealed. That's like water baptism. It makes you feel secure.

3. I've been cleansed. Bathing the body is an essential part of hygiene. Conversion, 'the washing of rebirth' (Tit 3:5b), deals with the grime of sin, and baptism reminds you that you are now to live as a cleansed person. Read Ananias's words to Paul at his baptism (Acts 22:16). They show how new birth and baptism belong together. We must not separate them. Once you're born again you qualify for it.

4. I confess Christ. New birth may be in the seclusion of your own room, but you can't have a 'private baptism'. In the New Testament it was in rivers and city pools. It's no 'hush-hush' affair. It's like an enlisted soldier putting on the uniform (Gal 3:27). You can't wear the uniform and be a secret soldier.

5. I am united with Christ in his death and resurrection, as in our reading (Rom 6:1–11). Think of the pool as the grave and your body as the corpse. What do you do with the corpse? Bury it. What do you do with your old life, with its sinful ways, now that you are a Christian? Bury it in the act of baptism. Christ rose again. Going under is followed by coming up. That's reassuring! United with Christ you rise to 'live a new life' (Rom 6:4). *Believe* for the symbolic act to be a reality in your life.

Conclusion

Baptism is not an 'optional extra' to salvation. It is a command of our Lord and Master. Complete the following verse: 'If you love me, you will . . . .
. . . .' (Jn 14:15).

Memorize: *Don't you know that all of us who were baptized into Christ Jesus were baptized into his death? We were therefore buried with him through baptism into death in order that, just as Christ was raised from the dead through the glory of the Father, we too may live a new life (Rom 6:3–4).*

Home task

1. Make a list of all those 'relics' of your old life that still cling, though you know that they can never be part of your new life in Christ.

2. Go over the list, and if you have already been baptized tell God concerning each one, 'That old thing went down into death when I got baptized.' *Believe* that God has now made you free.

3. If you have not been baptized, read Acts 22:16, and make up your mind to obey God. Meanwhile, renounce all those 'relics' of the old life on your list, believing that you are going to leave them all in the baptismal pool.

Introducing Study 6

BAPTISM IN THE SPIRIT

The Bible tells us that there is 'one baptism' into Christ. Being immersed in water is only one part of it. The other is baptism in the Spirit.

Although there have been great changes in your lifestyle since you were born again, you may be aware of a lack of power to live for Christ and witness for him in the world. Jesus' disciples, though they believed in him and loved him, were just like that before he left them. He gave them the promise of the Holy Spirit to come upon them and empower them. It happened a few days after he had gone back to heaven, on the day of Pentecost. What transformed men they became! Like the cross of Calvary, Pentecost is not just an historical event or a date in the church calendar, but a present reality. We are to *experience* Pentecost and its power just as surely as we have experienced the cross and its pardon.

Like water baptism, this is not an optional extra, but something God wants us to experience and enjoy at the beginning of the Christian life, as the early Christians did. This study is all about this wonderful promise Jesus gave us, and how we can experience it.

Baptism in the Spirit

Read Acts 1:1–9

Introducing the Holy Spirit

Of course, you have met him already! Your salvation and all the blessings that have followed have been his work. If we do not have the Holy Spirit we are not Christians (Rom 8:9). What Christ did *for* us, the Holy Spirit now does *in* us. He is not just God's power or influence. We are told not to grieve him (Eph 4:30), and you can't grieve an influence. He shares the Godhead with the Father and the Son (2 Cor 13:14). That's why we speak of the Holy Spirit as 'him', not 'it'. Now for Spirit baptism.

How baptism in the Spirit is described

Sometimes we read of the Spirit *coming upon* people (Acts 1:8), their being *clothed with power* (Lk 24:49), their *receiving* (Gal 3:2) or being *sealed with* the Spirit (Eph 1:13). Why *receive* the Spirit if we now *have* the Spirit? Receiving means *receiving in fullness and power*.

Is it once for all?

We don't need to be baptized in water every week, nor do we need a weekly baptism in the Spirit. But the first experience does need renewing or recharging, usually called being *filled* or *anointed*. Many fillings or anointings, but only *one* baptism. Peter was filled twice soon after his first filling at Pentecost (Acts 4:8, 31).

Our Lord's description

Jesus not only had the experience himself (Lk 3:21—22) but describes for us the Spirit-filled man: 'Streams of living water will flow from within him' (Jn 7:38). Such a man brings the water of life to others and quenches their thirst. God intends *you* to be like that.

What it does

Through this baptism the Holy Spirit will:

- ○ make Jesus increasingly real to you (Jn 15:26);
- ○ give you power and boldness to witness (Acts 1:8);
- ○ open up the Bible and make it living (Jn 16:13);
- ○ give you a new prayer/praise language (Acts 10:46);
- ○ make your praying effective (Rom 8:26);
- ○ lead you to right decisions (Rom 8:14);
- ○ set you free, especially in praise and worship (2 Cor 3:17);
- ○ fill you with God's love (Rom 5:5) and joy (Acts 13:52);
- ○ equip you with spiritual gifts (power tools) to do your job in the church (1 Cor 12:8–11).

You may not come into all this at once, but it's all there for you.

To serve the body

The purpose of this 'baptism' is not to make people think 'You're a great guy', but to equip you to serve Christ's body (1 Cor 12:7). The human body has many parts, each gifted to do its special job. So you are one of many parts in Christ's body, with a special job earmarked for you. (Remember 'election' in Study 3.) The Holy Spirit will equip you with the gifts you need. That's exciting! (See 1 Cor 12:12–13.) My foot is just as important as my hand, but not so prominent. Don't think that only the prominent members or the spectacular gifts are important (1 Cor 12:21–22).

How to receive

'If a man is *thirsty*, let him *come* to me and *drink* ... By this he [Jesus] meant the Spirit, whom those who believed in him were later to receive' (Jn 7:37–39). He gave you three things to do:

1. *Thirst*—a deep longing for God to meet you in this way. God creates thirst and satisfies it. If you're not thirsty, ask God why. If you have been filled, thirst for more.

2. *Come*—to Jesus, who baptizes in the Spirit, and *ask*. God gives to those who ask (Lk 11:13). But more than asking is needed.

3. *Drink*—that means to lay hold of the blessing by faith. Jesus says, 'Whatever you ask for in prayer, *believe* that you have received it [that's when you start drinking], and it will be yours' (Mk 11:24). Drinking is an act of faith (Gal 3:2). Praying is no good without faith.

Finally, *laying on of hands* is a ministry to help you to receive. The person laying on hands becomes a channel of faith for the imparting of the Spirit. Your teacher will be ready to pray for you in this way. Expect to be filled with

God's power. Expect to receive a heavenly language. Expect the rivers of living water to start flowing out.

Memorize: *You will receive power when the Holy Spirit comes on you; and you will be my witnesses* (Acts 1:8).

Home task

Under 'What It Does' there are nine things that you should expect. Write out those that are *not yet* true for you, underlining the statements, and copying out the scriptures. Then pray that God will bring you into this part of your inheritance. Remember, believing is receiving!

SECTION 2

Getting along together

(Studies 7–13)

You have seen that 'coming into Christ' is very much a personal matter. The Holy Spirit showed you your need, revealed the Lord Jesus to you and finally brought you to repentance and faith. That *could* all have happened without anyone else being directly involved. But once born again you are part of God's family, the church, and that means getting along with other believers. When someone joins the Forces, he has to 'sign on', which is a personal decision, but that leads to 'joining up', which means living with others. It's like that when you become a Christian and join the Lord's army.

Your personal relationship with God is of course very important. You will be learning a lot about that in Section 3 of the course. But in this section we want you to think about the exciting and very important matter of 'getting along together' in God's family. Most of your growth and development as a Christian will now come through your relationship with other believers. This will happen, not only because of what the leaders and people share with you, but because of what *you* share with them, for that will also help you to grow.

Introducing Study 7

THE COMMITTED BODY

When someone mentions 'church' what do you think of? The drudgery of attending some place of worship while others are enjoying themselves? Singing dreary hymns? Listening to boring sermons? Be prepared for a whole new 'think'. Real church is not like that at all. In the first place it is a commitment—not just 'going to church' once a week but discovering a new and joyful way of living in harmony with other Christians. It will be the most demanding and fulfilling thing you've ever experienced. Those who get most out are those who put most in!' As you explore the real thing you'll never want to opt out again.

The Committed body

Read Matthew 16:13–20

What is the church?

It is not a religious club (pay your dues and obey the rules), but a body of committed people who have *all* found a new togetherness with God and with one another. You can't get in without being 'born again'. The New Testament speaks of Christ as the head and the church as his body (Col 1:18)—i.e. people who share his life and come under his control. As the parts of a human body are varied, so are we. We can think of the church in two ways. Jesus said:

1. *'I will build my church'* (Mt 16:18) meaning *the universal church* for whom Christ died (Eph 5:25), i.e. all believers, regardless of 'label' or race, past or present. It has a unity that is invisible but real. Meet a Christian, even from another race or culture, and immediately there is a oneness.

2. *'Tell it to the church'* (Mt 18:17) must refer to a *congregation who gather together*, whether it's a city church (1 Cor 1:2), or a church in a house (Rom 16:5). It's a visible body of committed people. 'Church' in the New Testament is a company of 'born again', not simply religious, people. It never refers to a building. Jesus

promised that when the church met together he would be there with them (Mt 18:20).

What about denominations?

These have come through divisions in the history of the church, and were not in God's original plan. Jesus only founded one church, 'one body' (Eph 4:4), to which *all* true Christians belong. Your loyalty is first to Christ and his universal church, and then to the local church where he has put you. Open your heart to all believers and pray for them (Eph 6:18). Don't be put off by 'labels'. One day all will be united (Jn 17:20–21).

Any place for 'loners'?

Christians who don't have a church? Imagine my hand decides to 'go independent', and not receive signals from my head through my arm. And if all the other parts did the same, the body would be paralysed and die. 'Church' is not meetings or activities, it is *people in relationship*.

The New Testament doesn't say, 'Go to church and so be a good Christian'. It says in so many words, 'you Christians belong to each other' (see Rom 12:5), 'so get it together' (see Eph 4:2–3).

Giving and receiving

This is what the church is all about. If you want to receive in a big way you must learn to give in a big way, and we are not simply talking about money. That's what Jesus said (Lk 6:38). Start asking, 'What can I put into this?' not 'What can I get out of this?' and then you will get far more out than you put in. You may ask, 'What will I be expected to give?' We'll be answering that in greater detail in the following studies in this section. But first and most important, you must *give yourself* (2 Cor 8:5).

Wholehearted commitment

'The team won because of their total commitment' (sports commentator). This is what Jesus expects of his disciples (Lk 14:33). Didn't he give himself totally for us (Gal 2:20b)? Imagine a wife saying to her husband, 'I am fond of living with you but I don't like living with your body!' Your real attitude to Christ is seen by your attitude to his body, the church. You cannot be wholehearted to the one and half-hearted to the other (Mt 25:40; 1 Jn 4:20).

Commitment means faithfulness

That means: (a) *Being faithful in meeting* with your brothers and sisters to encourage them (Heb 10:25). (b) *Being faithful in sharing* your life, your time, your gifts, your money (Heb 13:16). Fellowship ('two fellows in one ship!') is sharing. (c) *Being faithful in submitting* to the elders and leaders who are shepherds of the flock (Heb 13:17). In a later session you will learn more about this.

Memorize: *For where two or three come together in my name, there am I with them* (Mt 18:20).

Home task

1. The New Testament tells us that Christ is the head of the church, which is his body (Col 1:18). Write down in your notebook what you think this means in practical terms (see also 1 Cor 12:14–27).

2. You have seen that being part of the church means

being wholly committed to your fellow believers. Write down in your notebook what you think such a commitment would mean for you. Pray over each point that God will help you be committed.

Introducing Study 8

LEARNING TO RELATE

We have been saying that *church* is all to do with getting along together, that is, relationships. Later you will see how essential relationships are if the church is to do its job. But in this study we will show that *love* is the cement that holds the building together.

It sounds so nice and easy—till you start doing it! Perhaps you think to yourself, 'If only everyone was as easy to get on with as I am!' If you think that, you don't yet know yourself—not fully. But you soon will—with the help of your fellow Christians! They will bring to the surface things deep down inside you that you did not know were there. You will learn to love them just as they are. And in the same way they will learn to love you. It is this kind of relationship that makes the church strong.

Learning to relate

Read 1 Corinthians 13

Introduction

Have you ever flared up when someone said something unkind about you? It wasn't really the unkind words that did it; they only caused 'something inside' to surface. It's learning how to deal with that 'something inside' and to get along with others that God will use to change you and make you like Jesus.

Holding together

Keeping 'the unity of the Spirit' keeps the church strong. 'United we stand. Divided we fall.' The devil, our arch-enemy, is always at work among Christians to cause division. Therefore, 'Make every effort to keep the unity of the Spirit' (Eph 4:3). How do we do that?

Love is the cement

The church includes all sorts. Some of your fellow Christians you would never have chosen as your friends, but God has chosen them for you, to shape you. But this calls for love. The cement that holds the church together is not natural or human love, but God's love. Love is his very character (1 Jn 4:7–8). When the Holy Spirit came to you he brought that love (Rom 5:5).

Love must be expressed

It's not just a warm feeling deep inside. It is not words without deeds (1 Jn 3:18). A young man in love with a girl who does not respond will look for ways to stir up a response. You must learn to do that to your brothers and sisters (Heb 10:24) by acts of thoughtfulness and unselfishness.

Love will be tested

It's not only your *actions* you need to watch, but your *reactions* to what others do to you or say about you. This is where love is put to the test. It's not just being kind to those you like, but learning to love those you don't like, who 'rub you up the wrong way'. It helps to remember (a) How patient God is with your faults. (b) Others have to put up with them too. (c) You tend to think of your faults as trivial and the other person's as big, but see what Jesus said (Mt 7:3–5).

Love always forgives

Think how Jesus expressed his love in this way on the cross (Lk 23:34). Where would we be without a forgiving God (Heb 10:17)? A forgiving spirit is what you must have in your heart, even before the other person says sorry. Jesus always taught that if you do not forgive your brother you won't be forgiven by your Father in heaven (Mt 6:4–15).

Handling the breakdown

Jesus knew that there would sometimes be a breakdown in fellowship between believers, and so taught us how to handle it. He spoke of two situations:

1. When you know it's your fault. (Read Mt 5:23–24.) 'Offering your gift' means praying, worshipping or serving God. God's acceptance of your 'gift' must wait until you get things right, so go first and make up the quarrel ('be reconciled'). Don't say, 'It's half your fault!' Simply confess your part and leave the rest with God.

2. When you believe it's his fault. (Read Mt 18:15–17.) Sometimes, in spite of how strongly you feel, it's fifty-fifty who's right and who's wrong, and so you don't get things right the first time. Taking 'one or two others along' the second time may help here. Even if it is all his fault your attitude must be right. You're not out to 'tear him apart' or 'show him up', but to *win* him—back to you, and back to the Lord. You must have a forgiving spirit and want to be one with him.

Who is responsible to act?

According to this teaching of Jesus, *you* are the one to act when fellowship breaks down—always! If *you're in the wrong or it's fifty-fifty,* you must go to the other person. If he's in the wrong you still go to him. You may say, 'But what about the other fellow?' Sure, he is equally responsible, but you don't have to answer to God for his obedience to this teaching, only for your own.

Memorize: *Be kind and compassionate to one another, forgiving each other, just as in Christ God forgave you* (Eph 4:32).

Home task

Find a quiet place, taking your notebook and ball-point:

1. List the names of those you have not forgiven. Ask God to bring them to mind. Decide there and then that you will forgive each one. It is often hardest, yet most important, to forgive those who are, or have been, closest to us, such as husbands and wives, fathers and mothers, brothers and sisters, fiancés or boy/girl friends. Call on God to give you a forgiving spirit, to drive all anger and bitterness out of your heart, and to fill it with his love.

2. Ask God to show you if there is anyone with whom you are not on speaking terms where it's *your* fault. Pray for God's help to put all such matters right. If you can go and see the wronged person do so, telling them you are sorry and asking their forgiveness. Otherwise write or phone. If more than an apology is needed, such as money to be repaid, do that also. Tell them that you are now a follower of Christ and are doing this to obey his word.

Introducing Study 9

THE COVENANT MEAL

Water baptism and the Lord's Supper (also called Holy Communion or breaking of bread) are the two great 'ordinances', or recognized religious ceremonies, of the church. We dealt with water baptism in the first section of the course, as it is very much part of Christian initiation or 'coming into Christ'. Now we are going to deal with this second ordinance, which I have called 'the covenant meal', for it belongs very much to this second section, expressing something very important about our commitment to each other, and our relationship together in the body of Christ.

The two ordinances of baptism and the Lord's Supper have certain common features. They both point directly to Christ, and are intended to remind us of what he did on the cross. Both illustrate different aspects of our present union with Christ by faith, which spring from the cross. Both are witnesses and proclamations of Christ by the believer. However, one essential difference is that water baptism, since it has to do with our initiation into Christ, does not need to be repeated, while the Lord's Supper points to our ongoing communion with Christ, and so we do it again and again. The truth that 'you are in Christ', which we find continually in Paul's epistles, is illustrated in water baptism. The corresponding truth that 'Christ is in you' giving you spiritual life and energy, is one of the great truths we shall see pictured in the covenant meal.

The Covenant Meal

Read Luke 22:7–20

The meal foreshadowed

The night God brought Israel out of Egypt a lamb was killed in every Israelite household, its blood sprinkled on the doorpost to save that family from the angel of death, and then the lamb was roasted and eaten. Every year afterwards they celebrated the Passover feast to remind them of their deliverance from slavery. This event in Israel's history was but a picture of the deliverance of God's people from the slavery of sin by Christ at the cross. It was while celebrating the Passover, as we saw in our reading (verse 7), that Christ replaced the Passover Feast with this covenant meal.

The first occasion

How Christ, the head of the church, observed this meal provides us with some keys as to how he wants us to observe it. Note these features:

   1. The day. It was neither Sabbath nor Sunday. Any day is suitable.

   2. The place. A private home, so no special place of worship is necessary.

3. The circumstances. An event of simplicity and infor-mality in an evening of conversational teaching.

The meaning of the meal

The two elements are the bread, representing Christ's body, and the cup (of wine) representing his blood. His body was given up to death and his blood was shed to save us. The bread, 'the staff of life', teaches us that we have life by his death. The cup teaches us that we have cleansing and forgiveness by his blood. Observing the supper is therefore:

1. An act of remembrance. Jesus said, 'Do this in remembrance of me' (Lk 22:19). He wanted the event of the cross to be always fresh in our minds. It is one way in which we say a big thank you. The cup is called 'the cup of thanksgiving' (1 Cor 10:16).

2. An act of confession. Since only those committed to Christ have a right to share in the meal, doing so becomes a confession of Christ as Saviour and Lord. By this means 'you proclaim the Lord's death' (1 Cor 11:26).

3. An act of participation or fellowship, with Christ. You don't just gaze at the elements, you eat and drink, and so participate in the body and blood of Christ (1 Cor 10:16). Jesus had spoken earlier of eating his flesh and drinking his blood, and so having his life (Jn 6:53–54). That happened at your conversion. But the covenant meal teaches us that we need to feed on Christ continually by faith, and find our nourishment in him.

4. An act of covenant. In your reading Jesus said, 'This cup is the new covenant in my blood' (Lk 22:20). You don't take the Lord's Supper on your own, but with those who are in the same new covenant. The loaf not only speaks of the physical body of Jesus that was crucified for us, but also of his spiritual body, the church, of which we are all members (1 Cor 10:17). In the meal we are celebrating that we are not only in covenant relationship with Christ, but also with one another.

Learning from Corinth

Turn to 1 Corinthians 11. Paul had to rebuke the Corinthian Christians because of the way they were observing the Lord's Supper. Some went hungry while others got drunk. By doing this they were despising the church and humiliating other believers (verses 21–22). They may have been having a communal meal, but instead of expressing covenant they were denying it. They were bringing God's judgement on themselves because they were not recognizing in their brothers and sisters the presence of the body of Christ (verse 29). As a result many had been taken ill, and some had even died (verse 30).

To avoid eating and drinking in an unworthy manner we must examine ourselves (verse 28), and put right anything wrong, especially in our relationships with other Christians.

Blessing and healing

It is often said that the Supper is 'a means of grace'. That is, it is designed by God to bring us blessing. But there is nothing magical or mechanical about it. There is no virtue in the bread and wine in themselves, even after they have been prayed over, and you don't receive blessing automatically by eating and drinking. It is only by faith that the life of Christ is imparted. By eating and drinking unworthily the Corinthians brought sickness and death on themselves. On the other hand it is possible to come to the Lord's table in faith and receive healing as well as other spiritual blessings. If you need healing look to God for it as you share in the Supper, for it comes as a result of his death (Is 53:4).

A few practical matters

As to how often we should observe the Lord's Supper, Jesus simply said 'whenever' (1 Cor 11:26), without saying how often. In times of revival believers may want it every day. This was the case after Pentecost (Acts 2:46). And they did it at home, which means it hasn't necessarily or always to be at church as in 1 Corinthians 11. Nowhere does Scripture require a minister or leader to be present. It could be a family affair, or after a time of fellowship with friends.

Memorize: *For whenever you eat this bread and drink this cup, you proclaim the Lord's death until he comes* (1 Cor 11:26).

Home task

Use your notebook to answer the following questions:

1. 'A man ought to examine himself' (1 Cor 11:28). What do you think that means practically? (Ps 139:23–24 will help you.)

2. What kind of things do you think would disqualify you from breaking bread?

3. If you come to take the Lord's Supper wanting to receive healing for your body or some other blessing in your Christian life: (a) What is the spiritual quality you most need (re-read your notes)? (b) How do you get it?

Introducing Study 10

YOUR LEADERS

God might have arranged things so that we Christians get all our instructions from God direct, and are responsible to him alone. But God has planned something very different. Though he does speak to us directly and personally, he also raises up leaders to act on his behalf. They have a very important part to play in teaching us God's will. The Bible often speaks of God's people as a flock and the leaders as the shepherds. How we respond to those whom God sets over us will have a great effect on our spiritual development.

Every believer has to learn to come 'under authority'. Only when we have learned this can we be entrusted 'with authority' over others. In this study you will learn about the leaders in the church, what they do, and how God wants you to relate to them.

Your Leaders

Read 1 Timothy 3:1–12

Order in the universe

It is a law of God's universe that in every area of life some people have to lead, and that means *authority*. All authority comes from God, and even governments are appointed by God (Rom 13:1). Where authority is lacking there is disorder and evil (Judg 17:6). In the church God raises up leaders and equips them to care for his people. We shall speak briefly of *travelling leaders,* and then concentrate on *local leaders*, as these are the ones with whom you will directly relate.

Travelling leaders

(Read Eph 4:11–13.) Note that these men have received gifts from Christ (verses 7–10) for special tasks. Apostles, prophets and evangelists all travel beyond their local churches. *Apostles* are spiritual builders like Paul, sent to found new churches and help them to grow strong. *Prophets* bring an immediate word from God to direct or correct what God's people are doing. Both are concerned with the building up and uniting of Christ's body. *Evangelists* reach out to bring new people to Christ, and train the churches to do the same. In New Testament times it was the travelling leaders, not some big church headquarters, who linked the churches and made them feel one.

Now we must look at the local leaders, that is, the elders and the deacons (Phil 1:1).

The elders

These are also called 'overseers', translated 'bishops' in our older versions, though quite different from what people understand by bishops today. Elders have to be mature and stable men, able to teach others. Though the apostles single them out and appoint them, it is God who makes them (Acts 20:28). Their task is to shepherd the flock of God (1 Pet 5:2). This means:

1. *Feeding*. Not only giving them food (i.e. teaching) but leading them into 'green pastures' (Ps 23:2) where they can learn to feed themselves from God's word. As one newly born into God's family, you will especially need feeding with the right food. Babies need milk, not a mixed grill! (1 Pet 2:2.)

2. *Tending*, as a doctor tends the sick. In every flock there are 'sheep' who are spiritually weak and sickly (1 Thess 5:14). Elders are committed to getting the sheep whole and strong. We have to learn to accept their remedies.

3. *Protecting*. Sheep are easily attacked by robbers or wild animals. Paul told the elders at Ephesus, 'Guard yourselves and all the flock' (read Acts 20:28–31). Elders must watch over the flock as those who have to answer to 'the chief shepherd'. Christ (1 Pet 5:3–4).

4. *Leading*. Shepherds in Bible lands always led the flock (Jn 10:4). It was the butchers who drove! Leaders have to take the lead. This means two things. They set an example for us to follow (1 Pet 5:3). They cry 'Come on',

65

not 'Go on!' Second, they give direction for the flock as a whole, and steer them on the right course.

5. *Ruling*. Sheep, if they want to be shepherded, must come under the shepherd's staff (Ezek 20:37), that is, under his authority. If the sheep do not submit, the shepherd cannot lead. So give your shepherd entry into your life, to correct and discipline you. This is not a harsh authority, but a loving rule to make you strong and secure.

The deacons

The word means servant. Deacons are a clearly recognized body appointed to assist the elders by serving the church in special ways, according to their gift. Elders are always men (1 Tim 3:2), but deacons may include women (Rom 16:1; 1 Tim 3:11 NIV margin, or NASB). Some would be gifted in administration, others to help the elders in shepherding and teaching. Deacons do not rule, or make decisions for the flock, but if they serve well they 'gain an excellent standing', leading to something higher (1 Tim 3:13).

Responding to your leaders

How we respond to them is how we respond to God who appointed them. We are commanded in Scripture to:

1. *'Respect' them and 'hold' them in the highest regard in love because of their work* (1 Thess 5:12–13). They have to work hard (verse 12).

2. *'Obey' them and 'submit' to their authority (Heb 13:17)*. Obedience is an act, submission an attitude. You may obey with a bad attitude. See how Jesus obeyed his Father (Ps 40:8). You might also disobey with a right attitude, but that would be in the unlikely event of a leader requiring you to disobey God, as happened with the apostles (Acts 5:29).

3. Be loyal and faithful. If you do the first two, this will follow. You won't criticize or murmur, or listen to others who do this (Jas 4:11; 5:9). If you have difficulty with anything elders say or do they will always want you to go straight to them and talk it out.

Memorize: *Obey your leaders and submit to their authority. They keep watch over you as men who must give an account* (Heb 13:17).

Home task

1. Read about the false shepherds in Ezekiel 34:1–6 and write down the six things that they did *not* do (verses 3–4), and the two things that they did that were wrong (verses 2, 4b).

2. Go through in the notes the five things that elders do, and write down against each why you need that sort of shepherding care.

Introducing Study 11

PLAY YOUR PART

Church was never intended to be 'a show' with a stage performer and an audience, plus a little bit of audience participation, such as singing hymns and saying 'amen' at the end of prayers. Church does not consist of 'priest and people'. It consists of people, all of whom are priests.

Already you have learned that the New Testament speaks of Christ as the head, and the church as his body. The purpose of your physical body is to express what your head is thinking, but this requires every part of your body to be working properly and obeying the signals coming from the head. It is just like that in the body of Christ. You are now a part of Christ's body, with a definite role to play, even though you may not be too clear as yet what that role is.

In this lesson you will learn that there is a spiritual contribution that you can begin to make, as well as human skills and abilities you can use, to glorify God as well as to serve and bless your brothers and sisters. A life of serving is the most fulfilling life there is.

Play your part

Read Romans 12:3–13

A special task

There are no spare parts in the body of Christ. You have been hand-picked and placed in that body for a special purpose. (Remember Study 3.) It is not simply that you might go to heaven, but also that you might serve God on earth (1 Thess 1:9).

Finding your place

Children playing a 'pretend' game often squabble over who's to be leader, and what part each is to play. In the church God chooses what each is to do (1 Cor 12:28). Your role will be suited to your gifts and personality. As you grow spiritually that will become clear, if not to you, at least to your shepherd. Meanwhile, whatever lies to your hand, or whatever you are asked to do, do it with all your heart (Eccles 9:10).

Learning to serve

More important than what we actually do is *how* we do it. Motive is what drives us, like the mainspring that makes the clock go. Our motive must not be primarily our own happiness and self-satisfaction, but a desire to *serve* our fellow Christians, and thus serve Christ. Of course God wants us to be happy and fulfilled, but when we make these things our goal we miss them. Someone said, 'I looked at the Lamb of God, and the dove of peace flew into my heart. I looked at the dove of peace and it flew away!' In Study 7 we saw that spiritual gifts were not given to us for our benefit, but to enable us to serve Christ's body. Jesus taught that serving others was the path to promotion in his kingdom, and that he himself had not come to *have* a servant, but to *be* a servant (Mt 20:25–28). Serving is love in action, a love that does not seek its own interests (1 Cor 13:5), but the interests of others (Phil 2:4). The Holy Spirit is able to fill you with that love (Rom 5:5).

You are a priest

In the Old Testament the priests were a special class of God's people qualified to offer sacrifices for the people who could not do that for themselves. As believers in Christ we no longer need a priest between us and God as the Israelites did, but are all made priests (Rev 1:6) and so have direct access to God (Eph 2:18). Being priests does not necessarily make us leaders, but does qualify us to offer spiritual sacrifices (e.g. praise, worship, service) to God (1 Pet 2:5).

Offering up spiritual sacrifices

Don't think to yourself, 'I could never do that'. You have begun to do it already without realizing it! Each time you prayed or thanked God on your own you were acting as a priest and offering a sacrifice. Start doing it with your teacher in these times together, and you will find it won't be a big step to do it in a cell or home group. There are few things that will thrill your fellow Christians more than to hear you participate for the first time. This in turn will give you confidence to open your mouth to share, testify, pray, give thanks or even exercise a spiritual gift in the congregation (1 Cor 14:26). As you grow the Holy Spirit will teach you when and how to participate under the authority of your leader.

Practical service

'If it is serving, let him serve' (Rom 12:7). This includes practical ways, as well as participating in meetings. If God's love is in your heart there will be many opportunities to meet the needs of others, e.g. moving house, baby-sitting, ironing, cooking, cleaning, gardening, shopping, providing hospitality or transport. Some have particular skills, e.g. plumbing, wiring, carpentry, decorating, typing, dressmaking. You will have great joy and fulfilment whenever you do any of these things out of love for others, for you will be serving Christ.

Memorize: *I tell you the truth, whatever you did for one of the least of these brothers of mine, you did for me* (Mt 25:40).

Home task

1. Go through the reading again in Romans 12. In verses 6–8 and verse 13 there are some eight or nine ways in which we may serve the body of Christ. List them under two columns in your notebook, first those that mainly refer to Christian *meetings*, and then those that could be

outside of meetings. Ask the Lord to help you to serve his body in both areas.

2. Make a list of the practical ways in which you think you would be able to serve others. There's no need to confine your list to the ways listed in the notes. Then ask God to fill your heart with his love, so that when the need arises you will be eager to serve, knowing that you are truly serving Christ.

Introducing Study 12

MONEY MATTERS

Of course money matters! It matters to you and it matters to God. That's why the Bible has so much to say about it. There's nothing wrong with money. We all find it pretty useful. But it's the craving some people have for more and more of it, the things they do to get it and how they then use it that can be evil.

In the world the man with money is usually respected as a man of influence, while the poor person is often despised. Though it's not like that in the kingdom of God, your attitude to money and how you handle it is seen as a test of your character. When Christ bought you for himself, he bought you right out, your possessions and all. You cannot therefore give yourself wholly to him without giving your money and your possessions. This means that you no longer own anything, you just manage it for God. One day he is going to summon all his 'managers', you and me included, and ask us to give an account to him of how we handled what he entrusted to us. This lesson is to help you to become a good manager, so that you won't blush when you have to give your answer.

Money Matters

Read 1 Timothy 6:3–10

Money can be dangerous!

The Bible speaks of money as being both an instrument for the kingdom of God (Lk 16:9) and 'a root of all kinds of evil' (1 Tim 6:10). That proves it isn't the money itself, but our attitude to it and how we use it that makes the difference. Here are some important safeguards:

1. *Don't love it* or get infected by the 'get rich quick' fever of the world. See what the reading 1 Timothy 6:6–10 says are the tragic spiritual results of wanting to be rich. Note too the remedy for this wrong attitude—learning to be content with what God provides.

2. *Don't make a god of it.* 'You cannot serve both God and money' (Mt 6:24). Whatever you put in the place of God is an idol. Don't be an idolator. Many Christians have drifted far from God because they put money and prosperity in that first place that rightly belonged to God.

3. *Don't hoard it up.* Men 'lay up treasure on earth' for security, but your treasures can be corrupted and your money taken from you (Mt 6:19). Instead of hoarding up what is 'so uncertain' (1 Tim 6:17) we should invest what we do not need in the kingdom of God. That's laying up treasure in heaven. That will not prevent us from making

adequate provision for our families (1 Tim 5:8).

4. *Don't run into debt.* Christians who are always running into debt are poor managers and bad advertisements for the kingdom of God. The only ongoing debt we are allowed is 'to love one another' (Rom 13:8). House mortgages are not debts, but watch those credit cards. Don't let them tempt you to buy what you can't afford.

Your money is God's

As a Christian you and all that you have belong to God. Your money is like the 'talents' (Mt 25:14 ff) Your Master entrusts you with it and gives you freedom to use it, but it is really his. He is testing you to see whether you will be 'faithful' (1 Cor 4:2) as his manager, or 'wasteful' (Lk 16:1). One day we shall have to give an account.

Learning to give

God is the greatest giver (Jn 3:16), and you are called to be like him. You don't do God a favour by your giving. You are simply recognizing that it's all his anyway. Some have a special gift of giving (Rom 12:8), not necessarily because they are wealthy, but because they have faith for this. Offering hospitality is an additional and valuable means of giving (1 Pet 4:9). How to give?

1. *Freely and cheerfully* (2 Cor 9:7). It's not meant to be like having a tooth out!

2. *According to what you receive* (1 Cor 16:2). Heaven estimates our giving by comparing what we give with what we keep (Mk 12:41–44).

3. *Systematically and prayerfully.* Not rummaging round in pocket or handbag at the last moment (1 Cor 16:2).

4. *Secretly.* Not making a big show of how generous you are (Mt 6:1–4).

Sowing and reaping

This is how Scripture likens giving (2 Cor 9:6–11). For every grain you sow, you may expect to reap many more. Generous reaping depends on generous sowing (verse 6), and you reap spiritual blessing, not just financial (verse 10). See what a generous return God promises you (Lk 6:38).

Tithes and offerings

Tithing is giving a tenth of what you receive back to God. Offerings were additional gifts—how much and how often is a matter of free will, hence 'free will offerings'. In the Old Testament tithes were for the support of priest and Levites. Similarly in the church, tithes are for the support of people (full-time shepherds or those who are in need) and offerings are generally for church expenses, special projects, or for the work of God outside your own congregation that you may want to support. When the people failed to bring their tithes and offerings into God's house to support his servants, God said they were robbing him (Mal 3:8–10).

Memorize: *Give, and it will be given to you. A good measure, pressed down, shaken together and running over, will be poured into your lap. For with the measure you use, it will be measured to you (Lk 6:38).*

Home task

1. How does Proverbs 3:9a describe our giving to God?

Write it down, and tell God that this is what you intend to do.

2. Read 2 Corinthians 8:1–7. It tells of the giving of the Macedonian churches in north Greece to help their brothers and sisters in need. Write down:

(a) how Paul describes their response (verse 9);

(b) what their own financial position was at the time (verse 2);

(c) how Paul describes their giving (verse 2);

Work out what would be a tenth of your income, and determine to put it aside for God. You don't have to be earning. You can start while at school, as I did, with pocket-money and money gifts.

Introducing Study 13

THE KINGDOM IS COMING

In this closing section on 'getting along together', let's take a look at the worldwide task that calls for such togetherness. It is summed up in one phrase, 'the kingdom of God'.

Only twice did Jesus speak directly of 'the church', but again and again he spoke of 'the kingdom'. What is the kingdom? Does it differ from the church? And what did Jesus mean when he told us to pray, 'Thy kingdom come'? Finding answers to these questions will enlarge your horizon, way beyond your own personal life or your own congregation, to see that you are part of a worldwide movement that is fast gathering momentum, and will end in total victory, just as God's word has promised. You can afford to ignore those lies of Satan that suggest you are part of a weak and failing cause. The fact is that you are part of a kingdom whose glory will one day fill the earth, as the waters cover the sea. This will inspire you to play your part in the coming of Christ's kingdom both by the way you live and the way you witness.

The Kingdom Is Coming

Read Matthew 28:16–20

Understanding the kingdom

In Scripture 'kingdom' is not so much the territory over which a king rules, as *the rule itself*. The kingdom of God is the rule of God, firstly over the lives of those who, like you, submit to his rule (Mt 7:21), and then over the whole world and its course of events. Here he overrules what men do to bring to pass his purposes in the earth (Dan 4:34–35). The church and the kingdom are closely related, but the kingdom emphasizes *the thing God is doing*, while the church emphasizes *the people he is using* to do it.

How the kingdom comes

You have seen that your conversion involved repentance for the past, and then coming under God's rule (Study 5). In this way you entered God's kingdom (Col 1:13). The coming of the kingdom means making the rule of God effective *in* the lives of men, and then making it effective *through* their lives, so that the will of God is done on earth (Mt 6:10).

The Bible does not teach that the world will be converted

or Christianized (Rev 22:11), but it does promise such a turning to God that nations become Christ's inheritance, and the ends of the earth his possession (Ps 2:8). Despite opposition and persecution the church in the New Testament became the most powerful movement of its day. So it will be throughout the earth in these end days. The crowning victory will be the personal return of Christ (Study 20). How, then, does God use his church to bring in his kingdom?

Kingdom lifestyle

Your new-found faith has brought you a new way to live. Your lifestyle has already changed, and will continue to do so. Certain practices, habits, ambitions and attitudes have dropped off, and new ones are forming, as you allow Jesus to rule. The influence of God's kingdom is not negative but positive. We are to be known because of what we do, not because of what we don't do. 'For the kingdom of God is... righteousness, peace and joy in the Holy Spirit'—qualities the world does not have but desperately needs. It goes on to say that such qualities are 'pleasing to God and approved by men' (Rom 14:17–18). This is a powerful way of influencing men, and happened with the first Christians (Acts 5:13). But there is something else:

Speaking boldly

Witnessing, i.e. telling others what Christ has done for us, is our joy and privilege, as well as our responsibility. The Holy Spirit was given to empower us to do this (Acts 1:8). The first Christians, though they had received the Holy Spirit, still prayed for more boldness, and were filled again with the Spirit for this purpose (Acts 4:29, 31). You will need to do the same. You don't need to know a lot or be able to answer difficult questions. Just to share what Jesus has done for you. The blind man that Jesus healed admitted that he couldn't answer the questions fired at him, but he added, 'One thing I do know. I was blind but now I see!' (Jn 9:25). There's no answer to that.

Memorize: *For the kingdom of God is not a matter of eating and drinking, but of righteousness, peace and joy in the Holy Spirit* (Rom 14:17).

Home task

1. How much has your lifestyle changed as a result of becoming a Christian? Write down in your notebook:
(a) Where you know God has changed you, e.g. habits, language, attitudes, ambitions, relationships, handling money, business methods etc. Thank God for each change.
(b) Where you still need to change. Ask God to make each one happen.
2. How is your witnessing going?
(a) If you have already witnessed to relatives, friends, workmates etc., ask God to show you the next step. He may want you to speak again, invite them to a meeting or give them a booklet to read. There may be others that you still need to witness to for the first time. Write down what you believe God is telling you to do.
(b) If you have not witnessed to relatives and friends, decide to make a start. Ask God to show you with whom to begin, to give you an opening and courage to take it. The first time is like breaking the ice. It's not so hard after that.
(c) Whether you come under (a) or (b), ask God to fill you afresh with his Spirit and make you bold.

Growing in God

(Studies 14–20)

A gardener noticed that one of the young plants in his greenhouse was wilting, while all the others of the same variety were thriving. When he tapped it out of the pot and looked at the roots he found that they were being attacked by a small insect. He destroyed the insect and the plant thrived.

As a plant draws its nourishment from the soil, so you draw your life from God. If there's something wrong with your spiritual roots, you won't thrive. This section is all about your life in God, how to make sure that nothing hinders its flow, learning how to nourish it day by day by having fellowship with God and feeding on his word.

It's the leaves, flowers and fruit of the plant that we see and enjoy. Because the roots are hidden we don't always realize how important they are. There may be many aspects of your Christian life that are more obviously interesting and attractive, but none that are more important than your spiritual roots. In this final section of the course you will learn how to keep them healthy and strong, so that you thrive as a Christian, and don't wilt.

Introducing Study 14

A CLEAR CONSCIENCE

The burglar alarm rang in the middle of the night at a certain business premises, and the police were soon on the spot investigating. But it wasn't an intruder this time, just a fault in the circuit.

Conscience is like an alarm bell that God uses to wake us up to the fact that something is wrong. Everybody has a conscience, but when it comes to registering what is right and what is wrong, different consciences may come up with different readings. Sometimes the bell doesn't ring when it should. Sometimes, like the business premises just mentioned, there is a false alarm.

What is conscience? How does it work? Why do different consciences sometimes tell their owners different things? Why is it that your conscience is troubled now by things that never bothered you before you became a Christian? This study will provide you with answers. Most important of all, it will explain why it is so important to keep a clear conscience, and how that is done.

A Clear Conscience

Read Romans 2:12–16

What is conscience?

It's an inner prompting to do what we think to be right and to avoid what we think to be wrong. It's an inner voice that is 'bearing witness' to you, 'accusing' you, if it thinks you are wrong, or 'defending' you if it thinks you are right (Rom 2:15). If you heed these promptings you have 'a good [or clear] conscience' (1 Tim 1:5). If you disregard them you have 'a guilty conscience' (Heb 10:22). Every human being, however primitive, has a conscience.

Is it reliable?

A head hunter may have no conscience about scalping a man from another tribe, but may feel guilty about killing a monkey, because he has been taught that monkeys are sacred. What is fed into the mind concerning what is right or wrong will determine how the conscience works. It's like a computer. Only if you feed it with the right information will it come up with the right answers. Since you have come to know God and to read his word, you will have a much clearer idea of what pleases and what displeases him than you had before.

What happened at conversion?

In the run up to your conversion the Holy Spirit used your conscience to make you feel guilty. It's his work to 'convict [or fully convince] the world of guilt' (Jn 16:8). It was his convicting that drove you to Christ. It was the truth of the gospel fed into your mind that enlightened your conscience, and brought about a new awareness of sin that you hadn't had before.

As you grasp more and more truth about the will of God your conscience will become more and more enlightened. This doesn't necessarily mean that you feel guilty about more and more things. It also works the other way round. Paul speaks of believers with 'a weak conscience' that was not fully enlightened. They felt guilty when there was no reason to (1 Cor 8:7–8). An enlightened conscience would free them from this. Remember the burglar alarm that went off when there was no burglar! How important it is to be 'filled with the knowledge of God's will' (Col 1:9).

Is a clear conscience important?

Very important. Our salvation is to set us free from condemnation (Rom 8:1), but if your conscience is not clear you will always be under condemnation. This will affect:

1. Your fellowship with God. You won't enjoy God's presence. It's like when you were a small child, you never felt comfortable with your parents when you had a guilty conscience.

2. Your faith. A guilty conscience and a strong faith just don't go together. Put the matter right, and at once faith is restored.

3. Your prayer life. A man came to Christ, and the Holy Spirit reminded him that as a boy he had stolen a bag of nails from Woolworths. Every time he tried to pray he saw a bag of nails! Only when he went back to the store and put the matter right could he get through in prayer.

4. Your desire for God's word. A troubled conscience can rob a person of his appetite for natural food; how much more for spiritual food.

5. Your witness. You may want to open your mouth to speak for the Lord, but Satan whispers, 'You have no right to witness. You're a hypocrite.'

If you set your alarm clock at night, but persistently ignore it in the morning, the time will come when you will sleep right through it. If a person wilfully goes on ignoring 'the inner voice', it will stop speaking. That means 'a seared conscience' (see 1 Tim 4:2).

How to keep a clear conscience

There are four important steps:

1. Immediate confession of sin. Do it the moment you become aware of sin (1 Jn 1:9). By praying, as Jesus taught, 'Forgive us our debts', we can keep short accounts with God. Then, when you have confessed:

2. Trust in the promise of cleansing. God is faithful and just to forgive and cleanse us (1 Jn 1:9). Our very consciences are cleansed by the blood when we confess (Heb 9:14). Then:

3. Obey your conscience. Do what you failed to do, or stop doing what you ought not to do. It's not enough to confess our failure. We must stop failing (Jas 1:22).

4. Continue to walk in the light (1 Jn 1:7). That means keeping open to God, sensitive to the Holy Spirit (that 'still small voice' inside) and ready to obey immediately.

Memorize: *I strive always to keep my conscience clear before God and man* (Acts 24:16—the words of Paul the apostle).

Home task

1. Make sure you have a clear conscience. If there is nothing troubling you, don't become 'inward looking' by searching for what isn't there! Just praise God for the blessing of being in the light with God. But if you don't have a clear witness that all is right, pray the prayer of David in Psalm 139:23–24 and, as God answers, take the four steps mentioned above.

2. You are trying to help a friend who says he has confessed his sin to God but has no assurance of forgiveness. Write down in your notebook what you would say to help him. You will find 1 John 1:9 useful.

Introducing Study 15

AMAZING GRACE

Ever stopped to think what is meant by the Old Testament (or covenant) and the New? God made the old covenant (or agreement) with the Israelites when he gave them the law. If they obeyed they would be blessed. If they disobeyed they would be cursed.

The new covenant that came with Jesus was a covenant of grace, not a covenant of law. That is, it was more about promises than commands. It spoke more about what God had done for men than what men could do for God. It promised to put inside men the desire and ability to please him.

Let's take a look at the home where Mother Law rules the roost. She's very strict, has little notices everywhere telling everybody what to do, and what not to do. She is always scolding, but never seems to encourage or help the children.

It's very different in the home where Mother Grace is in charge. Here the children are happy. They tend to be good and obey because their mother has that effect upon them. She encourages them with promises and helps them with their difficulties.

We all know which mother we would prefer to be under. But here's a strange thing. Even today there are believers who have come into God's family under Mother

Grace and then have taken themselves off and gone back under Mother Law. Whatever for? Little wonder Paul says to some Christians who did this, 'O foolish Galatians!' It's like taking a plant out of rich fertile soil and planting it in the desert. And we wonder why the church doesn't thrive!

What is grace? How can we make sure of always living under it? This lesson, one of the most important in the course, will help you to find answers.

Amazing Grace

Read Romans 7:1–6

Only two religions in the world

The religion of law and the religion of grace. Every religion, including the old covenant religion of the Jews (Jn 1:17) and modern cults like Jehovah's Witnesses, belong to the religion of law. It is one of do's and don'ts, by which men try hard, but without success, to please God. The gospel alone is a religion of grace, not emphasizing what we have to do for God, but what he has already done for us. Because the law depended on human effort it was 'weak and useless', and man had to be provided with 'a better hope' in Christ (Heb 7:18–19). He needed some power outside of himself (Rom 8:3). Although grace sets a higher standard than the law (Mt 5:27–28), it also works in us to enable us to live up to that standard (Phil 2:13).

> 'Run, John, and live', the law commands,
> But gives me neither legs nor hands.
> Better news the gospel brings,
> It bids me fly, and gives me wings!

What is grace?

It is the love of God in action towards those who are totally undeserving. It is 'something for nothing for those who don't deserve anything'. Because no man has ever deserved God's mercy, salvation had to be a gift (Rom 6:23). Even the repentance and faith required to receive that gift had to come from God (Acts 11:18; Eph 2:8). We owe everything in our salvation and in our Christian life to grace. It is God's unlimited supply of mercy, love, strength, wisdom, in fact, all we need, flowing freely to us (Jn 1:16). This makes us a joyful, praising people all our lives.

Back under law

The fact that some believers in New Testament times, having come into the kingdom through grace, then went back to a life of rules and regulations, was one of the greatest hindrances to the early progress of Christianity. The letters to Galatians and Hebrews, as well as part of Romans, were written to keep us from that. Even today it is still one of the biggest causes of deadness and defeat among Christians. Believers who are constantly defeated by temptation need to know that Paul never said, 'Try a little harder.' But he *did* say, 'Sin shall not be your master, *because you are not under law, but under grace*' (Rom 6:14). Grace *teaches* and *enables* us to say no to sin and to live a life that pleases God (Tit 2:11–12). To the Galatian Christians who were stupid enough to go back under law, he puts this question, 'Are you so foolish? After beginning with the Spirit, are you now trying to attain your goal by human effort?' (Gal 3:3). When we live by rules and regulations, and that always means human effort taking the place of the power of the Holy Spirit, we are back under law. We call this 'legalism'. We lose our freshness, joy and freedom.

Why does it happen?

For the same reason that many refuse the grace of God in salvation, and prefer to trust their own righteousness. It gives them something to brag about. They show off their righteousness like a street artist does his pictures, with a notice, 'All my own work'. See what God says about that (Tit 3:5). Grace takes away all cause for boasting and throws us wholly on God. Believers also go back under law because they never really understood what Jesus did at the cross. It came in our reading, so let's look at it.

There's a new marriage

In our relationship with the law we are likened to a woman who cannot marry the one (Christ) she really loves, until her present husband (the law) dies (Rom 7:1–3). A death has taken place (at the cross), Paul tells us, by which our union with the law is broken, freeing us to marry the One who rose from the dead, our Lord Jesus, and so become happy and fruitful Christians (verse 4). In other words, Christ's death not only loosed us from our sins, but also loosed us from the law, that old demanding husband. Now we are under a new husband who doesn't ask us to keep house on a pittance, but hands us his cheque book. What do we have to do? Believe completely what Scripture says about our married state—we are 'not under law, but under grace'—and learn how to make out cheques!

Enough—and to spare

'What was your fare?' asked the church treasurer. 'Sixty pence,' replied the visiting preacher. He went home with his bus fare paid. At the next church, knowing that the preacher had a financial struggle, they announced, 'Let us bless our brother with a love offering.' His fare had cost him the same, but he went home with his pocket bulging with bank notes, and a praising heart. Grace goes 'over the top' in generosity. It is God's 'abundant provision' (Rom 5:17). It is 'the riches of God's grace that he *lavished* on us' (Eph 1:7–8). Isn't that absolutely marvellous? God is such a great giver, but we have to learn to be great receivers. No matter what the temptation or testing—no matter what the opportunity or challenge—God's supply of grace is 'enough and to spare'.

Memorize: *He said to me, 'My grace is sufficient for you, for my power is made perfect in weakness' (2 Cor 12:9).*

Home task

This is to be an exercise in making out spiritual cheques.

1. Take a careful look at every area of your Christian life, and note down those where you feel you *greatly need* the grace of God. For example, it could be relationships—in the family, in the church or at work. It could be in your spiritual activities—worshipping, witnessing, praying, reading the Bible. It could be in your own daily life—speech, behaviour, inner thoughts. Don't be discouraged if the list gets very long!

2. Pick out two, or at most three, that you feel are the areas of *most urgent* need. Alongside each write down what is the provision that you want God to supply. Your list could read something like this:

(a) My mother—keeping my cool when she nags!

(b) Jim at work—grace to handle it when he mocks or talks smut.

(c) Discouragement in my Christian life—a tendency to be up and down.

3. Take these areas to God one by one in prayer, and tell him in your own words:

(a) That you are weak. That you haven't got what it takes.

(b) That you know that he has an abundant supply of grace for you. Name exactly what you want—self-control, courage, steadfastness, or whatever.

(c) That you now receive that supply of his grace by faith, that you thank him for the answer, and that you are expecting to see this need supplied.

Note: It would be wise not to add to your initial list of two or three. Just replace them as they get answered. You're in for an exciting time!

Introducing Study 16

TALKING WITH GOD

In Rome there is a sculpture of Moses carved in marble by Michelangelo. When he had finished it he was so overcome by its life-like features, so the story goes, that he exclaimed, 'Speak! Why don't you speak to me?'

Perhaps it broke his heart that he couldn't talk with that object of beauty he had created. The great longing of God's heart is to have fellowship with man. This is the purpose for which we were created. At the beginning we see God enjoying man and man enjoying God. Then sin came, and man ran away and hid from God. That fellowship has now been restored through our Lord Jesus and his salvation. But if you never meet, never write or never phone a friend your friendship fades away very quickly.

Because we have been reconciled to God we cannot take our friendship with him for granted. We must spend time with him. We must learn to listen to what he has to say. We must develop the habit of talking freely with him. Don't think about it as a duty you perform but as an experience you enjoy. Two people in love don't talk to one another because it's a duty but because it's a delight. An old church teaching says, 'The chief end of man is to glorify God and enjoy him for ever.' God wants you to enjoy him and he wants to enjoy you. This study will help to show you how.

Talking with God

Read Psalm 63:1–8

It's a two-way traffic

From the moment you responded to God in repentance and faith, a line of communication between you and God was opened up (Eph 2:17–18). To be in communication with God is a two-way traffic. It is not just you talking with God but it is also God talking with you. So let's think about:

Listening to God

A little intercom in my study links me with my wife in the kitchen, but we have to take it in turns to speak. I have to stop talking in order to listen. It's like that with God. Despite what Jesus said about it, many believers don't take time to listen (Jn 10:27). A wife, suing for divorce, accused her husband of not speaking to her in five years of marriage. 'What have you got to say?' asked the horrified magistrate. Meekly the husband replied, 'Well, er, I didn't like to interrupt...'! In your times of prayer does God ever get a word in?

1. *How God speaks.* He uses many ways. He may speak through Scripture, through spiritual gifts such as

prophecy, through conscience, through the counsel of a leader or through that quiet inner voice. Because you read the Bible or listen to a sermon does not necessarily mean that you hear God speak. It's when the Holy Spirit makes the words burn in your heart (Lk 24:32), and you feel you want to do something about it.

2. *It's friendship with God.* Moses met regularly with God, and God spoke to him as a man would speak to his friend (Ex 33:11). In this way Moses came to know God intimately (Ex 33:13). Isn't it wonderful to know that we can have the friendship of the Lord in the same way (Jn 15:15)?

3. *It's receiving direction.* God has not given us ability to direct our own steps (Jer 10:23). We are not to trust our own wisdom but to trust God for guidance (Prov 3:5–6). David always 'inquired of the Lord', that is, asked God for guidance, before making any major decision (1 Sam 23:2). That's the way to make right decisions. When it says, 'God said to David' it was not usually an audible voice, but an inner voice in his heart. In this way God is able 'to fill you with the knowledge of his will' (Col 1:9).

4. *It's receiving correction.* If, when praying about something you've planned to do, you become uneasy, it could be God waving a red flag. 'Let the peace of Christ rule [act as umpire] in your hearts' (Col 3:15). When your peace is disturbed it's like the umpire stopping the game. See how Paul's plans were corrected (Acts 16:6–7).

5. *It's learning to listen.* If you are not hearing from God it's probably because you're not 'tuning in'. God is always 'on the air'. How do you tune in? In your times with God learn to be quiet before him. Pray like Samuel, 'Speak, Lord, for your servant is listening' (1 Sam 3:9). But then, be still and give God a chance to speak. This is what Scripture means when it says 'wait for the Lord' (Ps 27:14). Older versions have 'wait *on* the Lord'.

Praying to God

1. A practice for all seasons. It requires no special technique, no special time, no special place and no special language. Old Bible English is not needed. 'Hear my prayer' is so much better than, 'Wouldest thou have regard unto the petition of thy servant'. Pray at all times (1 Thess 5:17), travelling to work or school, waiting for an interview, wrestling with an exam, in time of danger or temptation. You don't have to close your eyes or kneel. Notice the situation in which Nehemiah prayed (Neh 2:4–5). Prayer should be as natural as breathing. God wants you to share your life with him, and that means joys and sorrows, successes and failures.

2. Time set apart. Besides calling on him in a crisis or talking to him while on the job, it is important that you have regular time set apart when you give him your undivided attention. Jesus had such times (Lk 5:16), and he taught us to pray behind the shut door (Mt 6:6). Some only pray when they feel like it. But there's something in the Scripture called 'self-discipline' or 'self-control' (Gal 5:23). Often in the Christian life you have to learn to say no to yourself (Mk 8:34) by overruling your human desires and inclinations for something which you know to be more important. One evening I was preparing one of these studies when my wife asked if I would go for a walk in the park. I knew she had seen little of me all day, but I did so want to complete what I was doing. I said to myself, 'My wife is more important than my preparation.' Once I made the decision the rest was easy, and we enjoyed our walk together. It's often like that with God. Keeping a time set apart for God doesn't need to be legalistic.

3. How to draw near to God. It is good to start with praise and thanksgiving (Ps 100:4). In fact, always mix your requests with thanksgiving (Phil 4:6). God answers the prayers of grateful people. Don't be self-centred in your asking. Pray for others, not just for yourself. This is called 'intercession'. As you pray for others you will surely be blessed.

4. *The greatest of all.* 'If only I had some great intercessor to help me.' You have. The greatest intercessor on earth dwells within you to help you to pray according to God's will (Rom 8:26–27), and that ensures answered prayer (1 Jn 5:14). Trust him to guide you, inspire you and give you faith.

Memorize: *Do not be anxious about anything, but in everything, by prayer and petition, with thanksgiving, present your requests to God (Phil 4:6).*

Home task

Even if you have never done it before, take time this week to wait on God. Find a quiet place where you are not likely to be disturbed. Don't try to make your mind a blank, but just be still before God, asking him to speak to you, as Samuel did, and expect that he will.

1. Ask God if he has anything to say to you personally at this time, and then wait before him. Jot down what you believe he is saying, and do anything you believe he is asking of you. At the next session with your teacher share through what you believe God gave you. If he didn't give you anything the first time, don't be discouraged. Persevere in waiting on God and he will begin to speak.

2. Ask God to show you those he wants you to intercede for regularly. Again, jot down the names as they come to mind. Be prepared for him to give you some names you have never thought to pray for.

3. Bring those names to God one by one, and ask him to show you any needs they have individually. You may not hear from God about everyone, but list the things he does give against the names of the people concerned. Use that list as you pray.

Introducing Study 17

HANDLING THE BIBLE

It's sixty-six books, and yet it's one Book. It has many authors, and yet it has one Author. It is the oldest book in the world, and yet it's more up to date than tomorrow's newspaper. Already you will have discovered what a practical book it is, and how it speaks into your present life, and shows you things about yourself that you didn't know, as well as things about God.

The Bible is without doubt the most wonderful book in the world. Do you realize how privileged you are to possess a copy? Many Christians in other parts of the world would give almost anything to have a copy of their own. The best way to show your gratitude to God for the Bible, is not to preserve it in its nice cardboard box, or give it an honoured place on your bookshelf, or carry it around like a lucky charm. The Bible does nothing for you until you receive its truth into your heart and let it change you, as I'm sure you have been doing throughout this course. If in the past you have found the Bible boring or too difficult to understand, it will be very different now as the Holy Spirit begins to unlock its treasures for you.

This study will be a very practical one on *how to handle the Bible* so as to get the most out of it. It won't tell you how to master the Bible, but how to let the Bible master you!

STUDY 17

Handling the Bible

Read 1 Peter 1:22–2:3

The power of the book

From the moment you became a child of God you experienced the Bible's power. Verse 23 in the reading reminded you that your new birth was through the action of God's word. How do we explain its power? Although its words came from the lips and pens of men, those words were 'inspired' or 'God-breathed' (2 Tim 3:16), that means that as these men spoke or wrote they were controlled by the Holy Spirit (2 Pet 1:21). God was speaking through them. That alone explains how so many different authors from so many different countries, and living in so many different periods of history, could produce a book in which all the parts harmonize so perfectly.

Getting acquainted with the Author

This is the greatest thing that the Bible does for you. 'I've not met you before,' said someone to me at the close of a meeting, 'but I feel I know you. I've read so much of what you've written.' Acquainting you with the Author is the greatest thing that the Bible does for you as a believer. It's so much more important than filling your mind with information about God. The Holy Spirit makes God's word spirit and life to you (Jn 6:63). Every time you open the Bible expect to meet the Lord in the Scriptures and hear him speak.

The importance of right attitudes

If they're not right, no method you use will make your time with the Bible profitable. If your Bible reading is dull, the fault is not with the Book or the Author, but with the reader. The heart attitude with which you approach the Scriptures is the key to the time being profitable and enjoyable.

1. Clear the decks. Look at the above reading again and notice the things to be rid of before you come for the milk of God's word (1 Pet 2:1). All these things have to do with our relationships with others. Bad attitudes will affect your appetite for God's word. Rid yourself of them by repentance and confession.

2. Be hungry. 'Like newborn babies,' continues Peter, '*crave* (or have a hearty appetite for) pure spiritual milk' (1 Pet 2:2). If you are regularly opening the Bible with no spiritual appetite, and your reading doesn't stir it up, there's something wrong. Watch what else you are reading and viewing. Feed your mind on garbage and you lose your love for God's word. To be hungry is to be healthy. Notice how healthy the Psalmist was (Ps 119:131). If you're not hungry, ask God to show you why.

3. Be expectant. Don't just come hungry to the Scriptures, but come believing that your hunger will be satisfied. Jesus promised this (Mt 5:6). With God *believing is always receiving* (Mt 21:22). If you didn't receive, you didn't really believe, however much you thought you did.

4. Be submissive. Approach the Bible with a readiness to obey. Tell God that's how you're coming. Because they don't have a heart set to obey is the reason why many do not understand, or even misunderstand God's word. Because the Psalmist had an attitude to obey he could pray confidently for understanding of God's word (Ps 119:34). Obey the light and you will receive more light. That means, obey what you understand of God's will and you will understand more. Disobey, and your light (understanding) can turn to darkness (Mt 6:23b).

The practical needs

Of course, these apply to all the times you set apart for God, whether for Bible reading or prayer or both.

1. A regular time. Don't wait till you feel 'inspired' to read the Bible, but make a daily habit of it. I'm not legalistic because I take regular meals. My stomach looks for it and my health benefits from it! The Bible encourages us to meditate regularly (Ps 1:1–3) as well as to pray and praise regularly as Daniel did (Dan 6:10). It requires a little self-discipline at first, but in time it becomes second nature, like meal times. Note that if Job didn't have time for Bible and breakfast he chose Bible! (Job 23:12.) Many like to read and pray before breakfast. They find their minds are fresh and uncluttered, and that there's less chance of being disturbed by phone or door bell. Some get on better last thing at night. Sometimes Jesus prayed after the day's work was over (Mt 14:23), and sometimes he got up early to do it (Mk 1:35). You must choose the time most suitable to you.

2. A suitable place. This must be a place where you won't be disturbed. In the last scripture Jesus found 'a solitary place'. He told his disciples, 'Go into your room, close the door and pray' (Mt 6:6). We are not to make an exhibition of our devotions. Walking can be a very good way of meditating and praying, but it will require mental discipline to concentrate. It is an answer for those who can't get alone at home.

3. A reading plan. It is good to have a plan, but not to be rigid about it. Without a plan you may waste time wondering what to do, or become haphazard, jumping from one passage to another. An approved workman is one 'who correctly handles the word of truth' (2 Tim 2:15). Books of the Bible were written as books, and it is important to read them as books. But where to begin? As a new Christian your urgent need is to learn what it means to be a disciple (learner) of Jesus. So choose a gospel (Matthew, Mark, Luke or John) and go through it. Then take a short epistle, say 1 or 2 Thessalonians. Then go to an Old Testament book, perhaps the Psalms (Israel's prayer and praise book) or Proverbs, which is full of practical teaching on life. You need to be mostly in the New Testament without neglecting the Old Testament. But in your consecutive reading don't be rigid. If some other verse or passage comes alive to you stay with that for a while, then return to your consecutive reading. Let the Spirit lead (Rom 8:14).

4. A helpful method is to read and meditate. Have a notebook with your Bible. As you read slowly, ask God to speak to you (Ps 119:18). Keep on reading until something strikes you, then stop and meditate. That means to turn the words over and over in your mind as though chewing a mouthful of food to get all the goodness out of it. Twice the Bible tells us that we must learn to 'meditate day and night' if we want to be successful for God (Josh 1:8; Ps 1:2–3). The more you do it the easier it will become. Write down in your notebook the thoughts that God gives you. If you get through a whole chapter and nothing has struck you, go through it again. Persevere with it until the Book starts to speak to you.

Memorize: *Do not let this Book of the Law depart from your mouth; meditate on it day and night, so that you may be careful to do everything written in it. Then you will be prosperous and successful* (Josh 1:8).

Home task

1. 2 Timothy 3:16 uses the word 'God-breathed' or 'inspired by God' to tell us why Scripture is different from all other books. Explain what you think this means.

2. The same verse also tells us that Scripture is useful for four things. Explain in the simplest of terms what these four things mean and why they are important in the Christian life. Try to give practical examples.

3. Make a start on the 'read and meditate' method. Start at the beginning of Mark's gospel. Read till something strikes you, and then meditate on it. Write down the thoughts that come to you. Cover two or three different points that strike you.

Introducing Study 18

BEATING TEMPTATION

Temptation, as you will know, is not 'a little surprise' that Satan reserves for committed Christians. Everybody faces it. Perhaps it has troubled you to find that temptations have not eased off since you became a Christian. If anything they have probably increased. Perhaps you have thought, 'If I'm still tempted like this, can I be a real Christian? Has anything really happened?'

In the first place, temptation is not sin. It only becomes sin when you yield to it. In the second place, an increase in temptation is an encouraging sign that something has indeed happened. Your commitment to Christ has made you a threat to the kingdom of evil. Satan, the ruler of that kingdom, has therefore to redouble his efforts to drag you down.

But if God is all-powerful, why doesn't he see Satan off for good? Or why doesn't he rob temptation of all its power? One day he *will* destroy Satan for good, but he has not done so yet because he has a very important purpose in allowing us to be tempted. In this study we shall learn where temptation comes from, and that the grace of God that we studied in the last lesson is there to enable us to beat temptation. Learning to face it and conquer it puts something into us.

Beating Temptation

Read James 1:1–15

God and temptation

Verse 13 teaches that God cannot be tempted, and he does not tempt anyone. He may lead us into temptation (Mt 4:1), but he is always there, controlling and limiting it, and helping us to master it (1 Cor 10:13).

The rebel ruler

Since becoming a Christian you have become aware that you were in a spiritual battle. Before your conversion you were part of a rebel kingdom, serving Satan. Once he was one of God's angelic rulers, but he rebelled and was cast out of heaven (Lk 10:17–18). Satan's great aim, with his army of spirit beings (Eph 6:12), is to entice people away from God, and get them to serve him. He is called 'the tempter' (Mt 4:3). He does this by appealing to 'the cravings of our sinful nature' (Eph 2:1–3).

Satan's landing strip

The 'sinful nature' (called 'the flesh' in older versions) is that within you that does not and cannot respond to the

Holy Spirit (Gal 5:17). It is like an enemy landing strip within you that gives Satan an avenue to tempt you. Read again James 1:14. How do you deprive him of that landing strip? That old nature of yours cannot be reformed or changed, it can only be crucified through the cross of Jesus (Gal 5:24). When Jesus died on the cross that sinful part of you died with him. 'If it's dead,' you may say, 'it won't lie down!' Believe what God says and you will find that it is indeed dead. It was only as you believed that you came into salvation. It wasn't automatic. Just so with this—'count yourselves dead to sin' (Rom 6:11).

Liquorice all-sorts

Temptations are of various kinds. There is the temptation to do what you know to be wrong, and the temptation *not* to do what you know to be good and right (Jas 4:17). Satan uses various methods. As well as appealing *directly* to our appetites and selfish desires, he may use other people, as Potiphar's wife tempted Joseph (Gen 39:7), or as Peter tempted our Lord (Mt 16:21–23). Someone says something unkind, and you are tempted to give back in equal measure. He uses your success to tempt you to be proud, or someone else's success to tempt you to be jealous. He may use sickness, failure, disappointment, opposition, things going wrong to tempt you to discouragement, to accuse God of failing you. Like Peter when he denied Jesus, he may use your fears to prevent you from being true to Christ.

How to handle temptation

Here are six methods of handling temptation—and of making sure you come out on top:

   1. Develop a right attitude. Recognize that temptation, though it comes from Satan, is one of the 'all things' that

God works for our good (Rom 8:28). 'Consider it pure joy' (Jas 1:2). Phillips renders this verse: 'When all kinds of trials and temptations crowd into your lives, my brothers, don't resent them as intruders, but welcome them as friends!' It is 'a time of need' that makes us call on God for his grace (Heb 4:16). There's nothing like temptation to teach us how weak we are and how strong God is.

2. *Always be alert.* The devil is a great deceiver and knows all the tricks of the trade. 'Watch and pray so that you will not fall into temptation' (Mt 26:41). To be proud, careless or cocksure of ourselves is to be heading for a fall (1 Cor 10:12)

3. *Keep your nose out* of what God says is forbidden territory, that is, where Satan holds sway. To get involved in things of the occult such as spiritism, witchcraft, fortune-telling, horoscopes, ouija-board is to wander into enemy territory and risk being taken prisoner. You don't have to learn Satan's 'deep secrets' (Rev 2:24) just as you don't need to roll in the mud to know it's dirty!

4. *Don't play with fire.* Some Christians play with temptation as children play with fire. Don't walk into temptation. Mum caught Joe sneaking in with a wet swim suit after being forbidden to swim in a dangerous pool. When asked why he had disobeyed he replied, 'Satan tempted me.' 'But why did you take your swim suit?' 'I took it—er—in case I was tempted!' Romans 13:14b says 'Do not think about how to gratify the desires of the sinful nature.' Pornographic movies, girlie magazines, video nasties, certain records and anything that you know stirs evil thoughts and desires will mean walking into the devil's trap. Jesus said that you must cut off anything in your life that makes you stumble and fall into sin (Mt 5:27–30). Gouging out an eye or amputating a hand means taking drastic action to stop looking at or doing something that causes you to sin.

5. *Stand up and fight.* This is how you deal with most

temptations, that is, 'Resist the devil' and he will do the fleeing (Jas 4:7). But first you have to 'Submit... to God', that is, place yourself afresh under God's control. That puts you on God's side and then he will fight for you. Resisting the devil is not done with human strength or determination, but with faith in God's power. The fight is one of faith (1 Tim 6:12). By faith you stand your ground and by faith you 'extinguish all the flaming arrows of the evil one' (Eph 6:13, 16). When under fierce attack always call on the name of the Lord, and he will intervene to save and deliver (Rom 10:12).

6. *Flee for your life.* This is the way to handle some temptations. Don't stop and argue with the devil when he tempts you to 'sexual immorality (1 Cor 6:18); see how Joseph reacted (Gen 39:11–12). Or with 'idolatry' (1 Cor 10:14). An idol is any person or thing that takes the place in your life that is rightfully God's. Or with 'love of money' (1 Tim 6:10–11). Or with 'the evil desires of youth' (2 Tim 2:22) such as are mentioned in Romans 13:13.

Memorize: *No temptation has seized you except what is common to man. And God is faithful; he will not let you be tempted beyond what you can bear. But when you are tempted, he will also provide a way out so that you can stand up under it* (1 Cor 10:13).

Home task

Make a list of all the areas of temptation in your life that you have experienced since you became a Christian. Then:

1. Read again *'Keep your nose out'* on page 111. Are there any 'no go' areas in which you have been trespassing? If so, confess them to God, and make up your mind to have nothing more to do with them. If you have had a lot of involvement with the occult in the past share this with your teacher.

2. Look at those areas of temptation you have listed in the light of *'4. Don't play with fire'* on page 111. Are there any situations where you are inviting temptation? Write down what your decision is about each one in the light of Matthew 5:27–30. Ask God to give you grace to carry through your decisions.

3. Start thanking God for all those areas of temptation in your life. Remind God in your prayer that they are teaching you to draw on his grace and prove to you that he is greater. Keep thanking God until you find joy welling up in your heart as it says in James 1:2.

Introducing Study 19

THE BIBLE AND SEX

One thing must now be clear. The Christian life is not merely something that affects you for an hour or so on Sunday morning; it changes you through and through and touches every area of your life. It is not surprising, therefore, that a disciple of Christ has a different attitude to sex from those who believe in what is called 'the new freedom' and whose only rule is, 'If it feels good, do it.' The Christian's attitude is regulated by what God says about it, and he knows that God gives him grace to live accordingly.

Many people think that God is against sex. Not a bit of it! He thought up the idea, and created us all with our sex characteristics and desires. He 'richly provides us with everything for our enjoyment', and that certainly includes sex.

But sex was not only for pleasure. It was also to be the means by which the human race was to be perpetuated, and this required that children should be born into a loving and caring family relationship. So God laid down strict rules for the practice of sex, rules that are designed to prevent men and women using it solely for pleasure, without the commitment of marriage, and the loving, caring family that marriage makes possible. Failure to obey these rules is one of the greatest causes of unhappiness in our unhappy world. And it not only affects those who break the rules, but also those who are the innocent victims of their sin, such as little children in broken homes, too young to understand what it's all about. Not only do we please God when we are careful to obey what he has said about this, but we ensure the fullest enjoyment of this wonderful gift.

The Bible and Sex

Read Genesis 2:19–25

Sex is pure

This century has seen a sex revolution. No longer do children grow up with the impression that sex is 'a smutty little secret' that nice people don't talk about. Instead sex is now a 'free for all'. People cry, 'Be liberated' and 'Whatever turns you on!' Nothing is honoured and nothing is barred. Neither view agrees with Scripture. The Bible speaks freely and frankly about sex. 'To the pure, all things are pure' (Tit 1:15). Sex within marriage is viewed as something honourable and beautiful, so much so that God used it to illustrate his union with his people. 'Marriage should be honoured by all, and the marriage bed kept pure, for God will judge the adulterer and all the sexually immoral' or (in other versions) 'fornicators' (Heb 13:4). In a word, *sex is for marriage and for marriage alone*. The Bible never weakens on this point.

God's word on adultery

Adultery means a married person going to bed with someone of the opposite sex to whom he (or she) is not married, whether the other person is single or married to someone

THE BIBLE AND SEX

else. God knew that this would be the greatest threat to marriage and family life, so he included it in the Ten Commandments (Ex 20:14). Under the law of Moses the punishment for breaking it was stoning (Jn 8:4–5). It involves the breaking of solemn marriage vows made before God and men.

God's word on fornication

Fornication (involving 'the sexually immoral', NIV) has the primary meaning of sexual intercourse between a man and a woman who are unmarried. 'Sleeping around' or indiscriminate sex among unmarried people is so common as to be generally acceptable in the world.

'Come on, don't be old-fashioned, everybody does it.' The fact that so many indulge in indiscriminate sex is actually a good reason for refusing. God says, 'Do not conform any longer to the pattern of this world' (Rom 12:2), or 'Don't let the world around you squeeze you into its own mould' (Phillips translation). Draw on God's grace to stand up and be counted. The man of the world may outwardly scoff yet inwardly admire Christians who have the courage to stand by their convictions.

God's word on homosexuality

We are talking about men having sexual relations with men, or women having such with women (called 'lesbianism'). It is expressed today in such organizations as 'The Gay Liberation Movement'. God hates all such forms of unnatural sex (Lev 18:22–23). We must hate them too, while having compassion towards those caught up in them. God overthrew the cities of Sodom and Gomorrah for the sin of homosexuality ('sodomy'). In the New Testament God had not changed his mind about this (Rom 1:26–27). Practising homosexuals are among those who will not inherit the kingdom of God (1 Cor 6:9–10), but there is no truth in the saying, 'Once a homosexual always a homosexual'. Some of the Corinthian believers had been set free from this practice (verse 11). God is still setting homosexuals free today.

A word about flirting

This means to 'play at courting or making love with no serious intention of marriage'. Even when this does not involve 'petting' (kissing and caressing) simply for kicks, it is still selfish and unworthy of a Christian. Flirting has been described as 'attention without intention'. Love is too serious for play-acting. One person may be play-acting and the other deadly serious. This can result in one being deeply wounded, if not scarred for life. Paul told Timothy how to treat the younger women in the church (1 Tim 5:2). If single, be wise and don't get locked into an exclusive friendship with a member of the opposite sex until you know you are meant for each other.

A word about courting

If you are unmarried God says, 'Do not be yoked together with unbelievers' (2 Cor 6:14), that is, don't marry someone not 'born again'. Marriage is 'a yoke' because it compels two to walk together. If you are already married God can use you to bless your unbelieving partner (1 Cor 7:14).

Courting develops the relationship in preparation for marriage. Petting obviously has a part to play, but the rule 'no sex outside of marriage' still applies. Going to bed together before marriage (pre-marital intercourse) is still fornication. So a couple determined to please God will refrain from 'heavy petting', that is, caressing the intimate parts of your partner's body, which is the build-up to sexual intercourse, for that would be walking into strong temptation. God's ideal is for the bride to present herself to her husband on the wedding day as a 'pure virgin' (2 Cor 11:2). If your relationship is in the will of God, you don't need a trial run to find out if you're 'sexually adjusted' to each other.

A word about self-control

Sex desire is like an inner fire (Prov 6:27–29). To have a log fire in the house may be beautiful if it's burning safely in the grate, but if it's burning merrily on the lounge floor the house could be burned down. Self-control keeps the fire in the grate, that is to say, keeps sex *in the right place for the right person at the right time*. Whether you are single, engaged, married, widowed or divorced you will always need the grace of self-control. The world says that to try to restrain your sex urges is to do yourself an injury. What nonsense! God commands us: 'Be self-controlled... be holy' (1 Pet 1:13–15).

One of the world's substitutes for self-control is masturbation. This means the stimulation of one's own sex organs to attain that climax of sexual excitement that God intended for the marriage act. This is not to say that masturbation is a sin like fornication, but it *is* sinful when accompanied, as is so often the case, by sexual fantasies and impure thoughts. It *is* sin when it masters you and you cannot 'kick' the habit (1 Cor 6:12), As a single young man Jesus had to face the same sex desires as we do. I cannot think that he chose the easy way of self-indulgence that some psychiatrists recommend, rather than drawing on the grace that teaches us to say no (Tit 2:11–12). Sex energies don't have to have a sexual outlet. They can be redeployed in the service of God and of others. You don't *have* to masturbate. Countless Christians have found that the grace of self-control is a better way. Having taken that

119

way, don't give up because of a failure. The grace of God
waits to restore you (Mic 7:8).

Memorize: *It is God's will that you should be holy; that
you should avoid sexual immorality; that
each of you should learn to control his own
body in a way that is holy and honourable*
(1 Thess 4:3–4).

Home task

The battle with sex temptation is really a battle in the
mind. If you win there, you end up a winner.

1. This battle is described in 2 Corinthians 10:3–5. It
speaks of 'strongholds' of the mind that must be demoli-
shed, and the 'weapons' that can do the job. Go over your
thought life and jot down what are the strongholds, the
places where pride, jealousy, uncleanness etc. hold sway.
Then take a look at your spiritual weapons, such as the
prayer of faith and speaking the word of God in faith. Aim
the weapon of prayer at these strongholds and start demo-
lishing them. Speak out in faith God's promises as you
pray—'Sin shall not be your master' (Rom 6:14). 'The one
who is in you is greater than the one who is in the world'
(1 Jn 4:4). 'Thanks be to God! He gives us the victory
through our Lord Jesus Christ' (1 Cor 15:57).

2. Access to the mind is through 'eyegate' and 'eargate'.
Take another careful look at the books and magazines
you read, the videos or television programmes you view
and the records you listen to. Get rid of whatever is being
used to set up strongholds. 'If in doubt, chuck it out!' Job
had a problem with 'eyegate'. If you have a similar problem
you can deal with it as he did (Job 31:1).

Introducing Study 20

THE GRAND FINALE

Rejected by the Jewish nation, condemned to crucifixion by the Roman authority, passing through the jeering crowds to a place of execution—that was the last the world saw of Jesus of Nazareth. He did rise again three days later, of course, but he only appeared to his followers. Then he went back to heaven. But he left his disciples a promise: 'I'll be back!'

The Saviour of the world, the Head of the church, the King of the nations has yet to be publicly owned and glorified by his Father before the whole universe.

> Look, he is coming with the clouds, and every eye will see him, even those who pierced him; and all the peoples of the earth will mourn because of him (Rev 1:7).

What a day! Both for him and for those who took his side when all the world was against him. The return of Jesus is the supreme hope of the Christian. It is mentioned 318 times in the 260 chapters of the New Testament, that is, an average of once in every twenty-five verses. In a world scared about the future, the Christian lifts up his head. If the outlook appears grim, the uplook is glorious! The best is yet to come. One day soon the world will acknowledge Jesus as King of kings and Lord of lords. What will his coming mean for the watching believer? For the careless Christian? For the Christ-rejector? For the world? For the future? That's the theme of our final study.

The Grand Finale

Read 2 Peter 3:3–13

The prophetic scriptures

A big proportion of the Bible is prophecy, teaching us about things to come, and helping us to understand God's future purposes. It is not 'history written in advance' but a series of future landmarks. Some we may only recognize as they happen (Mt 24:32–33). It's like looking for landmarks on a journey. You exclaim, 'There's the highrise flats. We're on course!' The prophetic scriptures are 'a light shining in a dark place, until the day dawns' (2 Pet 1:19). They give us guidance and assure us that everything is under control. The final goal of Bible prophecy is the *return of Christ*. Beyond all other expectations, this is the hope of the Christian (Tit 2:13).

The return of Christ

Before Jesus left his disciples to go back to heaven he said, 'I will come back and take you to be with me' (Jn 14:3). He was not referring to coming back to them in resurrection, or coming to them in the person of the Holy Spirit, or coming to them at death. The moment Jesus had gone back to heaven two angels informed his disciples, 'This same Jesus, who has been taken from you into heaven, will come back in the same way you have seen him go into heaven' (Acts 1:11), that is, personally, visibly, physically. Watch for references in Scripture to his 'coming', 'appearing', 'revelation'. Or to 'the day of God', 'the day of the Lord', 'the day of Christ', or simply 'the day'. All these expressions are used to describe the return of Christ.

A new age

The first coming of Jesus ended the age of law and brought in the age of grace (Jn 1:17). The second coming of Jesus will end the age of grace, with its opportunity to believe and be saved, and usher in a new age. Jesus spoke of 'this age' and of 'the age to come' (Mt 12:32). As we saw in our reading in 2 Peter 3, it will mean that this present world, once destroyed by water (The Flood), will be destroyed by fire. There will be new heavens and a new earth in which righteousness dwells. It will mean a new order of existence for which we will require new bodies.

A day of resurrection

At Christ's return those who have died as believers will rise from the dead with a resurrection body like that of Jesus (Phil 2:20–21). Believers still alive will be instantaneously changed (1 Cor 15:51–52) and with their resurrection bodies be 'caught up...to meet the Lord in the air' (1 Thess 4:17). This is sometimes called 'the rapture'. There will also be a resurrection of the ungodly. They will rise to be judged and condemned (Jn 5:28–29).

A day of judgement

All men are accountable to God. The accounting day is fixed for the return of Christ (Acts 17:31). (a) *For believers.*

Having received Christ, believers will not be judged on that issue of salvation, but will come before 'the judgement seat of Christ' to account for 'the things done while in the body, whether good or bad' (2 Cor 5:10). As a result we will receive rewards or suffer loss (1 Cor 3:12–15). (b) *For unbelievers.* Men will *not* be condemned for being in the dark, only for having refused God's way into the light (Jn 3:19). For this they will suffer eternal 'death' (Rom 6:23).

A royal display

Every bridegroom wants to show off his bride for she is his glory. At his return Jesus will be 'glorified in his holy people' (2 Thess 1:10). The kingdom will have finally come. He will reign supreme, with all his enemies subdued. Read Revelation 19:6–8, and begin to sense the jubilation of that coming hour of triumph for Jesus and for you.

The effect of this hope

Though Jesus gave us 'signs' or pointers to the nearness of his coming, he also stated that only God the Father knew exactly when he would return (Mt 24:36, 42). Scripture tells us his coming will be like that of a thief (1 Thess 5:2–3), requiring us to be continually alert lest we lose our spiritual valuables. The hope of Christ's coming requires us to live disciplined and holy lives and to purify ourselves from anything that could cause us shame when he comes (1 Jn 2:28, 3:2–3). To summarize, if you are gripped by this hope it will make you eager to serve Christ, ready to suffer for him and watchful to please him in everything.

Memorize: *What kind of people ought you to be? You ought to live holy and godly lives as you look forward to the day of God and speed its coming* (2 Pet 3:11–12).

Home task

Read the parable of the pounds (or minas) in Luke 19:11–26. Using the following questions interpret the parable, applying it to yourself.

1. Each of the servants received an equal portion of their master's wealth. As a servant of Christ, what would you consider is the pound (mina) that he has given you?

2. How are you now using your Master's pound so as to make it gain more?

3. Notice the three types of person whom the King dealt with on his return:

(a) the faithful servants (verses 16–19);
(b) the unfaithful servant (verses 20–26);
(c) the rebellious citizens (verses 14, 27).

Explain whom these three classes represent in terms of individuals whom Christ will deal with at his return.

4. The two classes that need to concern you are the first two. Write down where you find temptation to be unfaithful to Christ (e.g. laziness, unbelief, self-will, discouragement, 'I'm no good' attitude etc.), and claim in prayer God's promised 'grace to help us in our time of need' (Heb 4:16). Determine before God that you will be among those who receive Christ's 'Well done, good and faithful servant' when he returns.

Going On God's Way

by Arthur Wallis

A practical course for spiritual growth, following on from the initial volume *Living God's Way*.

It is all too easy to enter the Christian life with joy and strength of purpose, only to find that the pressures of the world dull your earlier fire and lead you to settle for something less than an effective, vibrant Christian life.

This course is designed to help you ensure that spiritual growth is a reality in your life and your church. Eighteen studies cover three main areas of Christian reality: the new person; growing strong; and living in the world. Practical, relevant, biblical – and ideal for individual or group use – the course has been worked out in a church situation and prepared by one of Britain's leading Christian teachers.

Arthur Wallis has written eight books over a span of three decades, and is internationally renowned for his Bible teaching ministry.

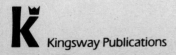

Kingsway Publications

Pray in the Spirit

by Arthur Wallis

In this book Arthur Wallis concentrates on the ministry of the Holy Spirit in relation to prayer, and investigates the full meaning of the apostle's injunction to 'pray in the Spirit'.

He analyses the spiritual and practical difficulties we encounter, and shows how the Holy Spirit helps us in our weakness and makes up for all our deficiencies. We are encouraged to yield ourselves completely to Him, allowing Him to pray through us.

As we enter into the 'deep things of God' unfolded here we shall discover a new power and effectiveness in our Christian lives.

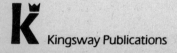

Kingsway Publications